SOCIAL GRACES

Town&Country

SOCIAL GRACES

— • —

WORDS OF WISDOM ON CIVILITY
IN A CHANGING SOCIETY

— • —

EDITED BY JIM BROSSEAU

HEARST BOOKS
A DIVISION OF STERLING PUBLISHING CO., INC.
NEW YORK

Copyright © 2002 by Hearst Communications, Inc.

Design: Esther Bridavsky
Illustrations: Chesley McLaren

Library of Congress Cataloging-in-Publication Data
Town & Country's social graces : words of wisdom on civility in a
changing society / edited by Jim Brosseau.
     p.cm.
ISBN 1-58816-080-7
Etiquette. I. Title: Town and country's social graces. II. Brosseau, Jim.
III. Town & country (New York, N.Y.)

BJ1853.T68 2002
395—dc21   2001039863

10   9   8   7   6   5   4   3   2   1

Published by Hearst Books,
A Division of Sterling Publishing Company, Inc.
387 Park Avenue South, New York, N.Y. 10016

Town & Country and Hearst Books are trademarks owned by
Hearst Magazines Property, Inc., in USA, and
Hearst Communications, Inc., in Canada.

Distributed in Canada by Sterling Publishing
c/o Canadian Manda Group, One Atlantic Avenue, Suite 105
Toronto, Ontario, Canada M6K 3E7
Distributed in Australia by Capricorn Link (Australia) Pty. Ltd.
P.O. Box 704, Windsor, NSW 2756 Australia

Printed in the United States of America

ISBN: 1-58816-080-7

ACKNOWLEDGMENTS

———•———

THE EDITOR WISHES TO THANK THE WRITERS of this anthology, whose work graced the pages of *Town & Country* magazine and now graces these pages; *Town & Country* editor in chief Pamela Fiori, a believer in the word "yes" who gave the *Social Graces* column the green light; the rest of his *Town & Country* colleagues, especially Mary Shanahan and Agnethe Glatved; the staff of Hearst Books, in particular Jacqueline Deval, Maryanne Bannon and the ever patient Elizabeth Rice; designer Esther Bridavsky, illustrator Chesley McLaren, and copyeditor Brenda Goldberg; and his family, especially Philip and Genevieve.

CONTENTS

Introduction *by Pamela Fiori*   10

CHAPTER I Modern Times

Privacy . . . or What's Left of It *by Jay McInerney*   16

On Accountability *by Ron Powers*   20

Play Fair *by Heywood Hale Broun*   24

The Etiquette of E-Mail *by Owen Edwards*   28

The Sound and My Fury *by William Norwich*   32

Rekindling the Holiday Spirit *by Sally Quinn*   36

Smugly American *by Andrew Nagorski*   40

The Right of Way *by Owen Edwards*   45

CHAPTER II Little Things Mean a Lot

On Being a Gentleman *by David Brown*   52

Don't Forget the Flowers *by Cokie Roberts & Steven V. Roberts*   56

Dressing for Dinner *by John Mariani*   60

Respecting Our Elders *by Anne Taylor Fleming*   64

Say "Thank You" *by Catherine Calvert*   67

CHAPTER III Family Affairs

Keeping It in the Family *by Sue Miller*   74

Nagging Habits *by Susan Dundon*   78

A Single Parent's Say *by Véronique Vienne*   82

Missing the Point *by Patricia Beard*   86

Grand (Parent) Expectations *by Anne Bernays*   90

With All Due Respect *by Stacey Okun*   94

Whose Wedding Is It, Anyway? *by Susan Dundon*   99

CHAPTER IV A Word's Worth

Curses! *by Jonathan Alter*   106

Put It in Writing *by Helen Gurley Brown*   111

What's in a Name? *by Deirdre McNamer*   115

Just Say You're Sorry *by Deborah Tannen*   119

When Money Squawks *by David Brooks*   123

In Memoriam *by Jim Brosseau*   127

CHAPTER V Honor Thy Neighbor

Rules for Renovation *by Stephen Henderson*   134

The Boor of the Grease Paint *by Wendy Wasserstein*   138

When the Tail Wags the Dog *by Marshall de Bruhl*   142

Cellular Phonies *by Pearson Marx*   146

What's So Good About Gossip? *by Molly Haskell*   150

Don't Waste Time *by Craig Wilson*   154

CHAPTER VI A Touch of Tolerance

Spiritually Speaking *by Stephen Henderson*   160

Sobering Thoughts *by Debbie Seaman*   164

Political Stomping *by Peggy Noonan*   168

The Measure of a Woman *by Véronique Vienne*   172

Straight from the Heart *by Lauren Picker*   176

Fish Out of Water *by Charles Dubow*   181

Widow's Pique *by Charlotte Y. Salisbury*   186

CHAPTER VII Life of the Party

Speak Easy *by Diana McLellan*   192

Don't Forget the Punch Line *by David Brown*   197

Utterly Shameless *by Letitia Baldrige*   201

Jetiquette *by Lyle Crowley*   205

Long Live the Gracious Host *by Nancy Tuckerman*   209

Please Don't Interrupt *by Barbara Howar*   214

CHAPTER VIII They Also Serve

Give Me the Civil Life *by Anne Taylor Fleming*   220

A View from the Fridge *by Anthony Bourdain*   224

Some Holiday Tips *by Francine Maroukian*   228

More Than Just the Nanny *by Janet Carlson Freed*   232

The Forgotten Groom *by Charles Dubow*   236

CHAPTER IX What Grace Does

Something in the Way She Moves *by Owen Edwards*   242

There Is Nothing Like a Dane *by Jane Smiley*   245

When Daddy Was King *by Frank Langella*   249

Invisible Grace *by Owen Edwards*   253

INTRODUCTION

SHORTLY AFTER I BECAME EDITOR IN CHIEF OF *Town & Country*, I became painfully aware of just how strongly civility was under assault. Forgotten thank-yous and the indiscriminate use of longshoreman's parlance—especially by people who should know better—had become the common currency of social interaction. Expressions once bleeped on television were uttered freely and without the blink of an eye. Obscene language began routinely appearing on the pages of national magazines and newspapers. Worse, far worse, our behavior toward each other was disintegrating rapidly. Somebody, I felt, had to speak up, and who better than *Town & Country*? The magazine began life in 1846 and has been America's social chronicler and arbiter of taste longer than any other publication. It was time for *Town & Country* to throw down the gauntlet.

So, in 1995, we introduced a new department called "Social Graces," to address this erosion of decorum. It would be neither a traditional etiquette column nor a repository for nostalgia (no use pining for the way things used to be). Rather, it would be a way of exploring the breakdown of civility through a thoroughly modern prism and offering unstuffy advice on maintaining one's manners, not to mention one's patience, in a world with little time for either.

We turned to some of the country's most eloquent and astute social observers, hoping they would have the same strong feeling we had. And they did, powerfully. Starting with Jay McInerney's fine first essay, "Privacy . . . or What's Left of It," we looked at subjects as varied as "Rekindling the Holiday Spirit" by Sally Quinn, and "Keeping It in the Family" by Sue Miller. And Molly Haskell asked "What's So Good About Gossip?" If these titles sound faintly old-fashioned, be assured that the point of view within the essays is anything but. One of my favorites is about the flagrant use of cell phones in public by people who simply cannot keep their business to themselves. (We even coined the phrase "Cellular Phonies.") Another essay points out the arrogance of certain individuals who, once in the driver's seat (literally), believe they have "The Right of Way."

Why should we care about good manners and proper behavior in the first place? Because they smooth the path. Civil obedience, if you will, makes life infinitely easier and more pleasant for everybody concerned. If you don't believe me, just observe the incredible effectiveness of people who know how to treat their fellow man or woman. Or how a dollop of consideration garners heaps of gratitude. Unlike bravery, kindness doesn't win awards. But, deep down, I believe that those who try their best to make life on earth a better place will be the first in line at Heaven's gate— and not because they cut in.

One such person is the editor of this anthology, Jim Brosseau. From the start, Jim took on *Social Graces* with unusual enthusiasm and even wrote one of the best essays—on how to deliver a sensitive eulogy. He and I had a wonderful time coming up with most of the ideas and then finding the writers to do them justice. More than a collaboration, it was a conspiracy to restore civility to its rightful place. I can't think of a better partner in this worthy mission than the socially gracious Jim Brosseau.

In reading these essays, I hope you will find wisdom as well as wit. So put up your feet—if you're not in public, of course—and have a good time. Above all, remember those three little magical words: "please" and "thank you."

Pamela Fiori
Editor in Chief
Town & Country

I
MODERN TIMES

*In the brazen new world, the ease of
communication and the speed of travel can leave behind
something called the human element.*

Privacy... or What's Left of It

by Jay McInerney

few years ago some letters disappeared from my desk. Being absent-minded and an atrocious slob, I was able to imagine that I had misplaced the folder somehow, until I happened to be grimacing my way through an advance copy of a fairly unreadable book and found some readable and strangely familiar sentences scattered about the page. The writer of the book was an acquaintance of mine, and there was no question that only the person in possession of my correspondence could have come up with the six or seven sentences that I eventually recognized. Hardly the most dramatic case of robbery or plagiarism in recent history, but I admit I was appalled at the so-called author. Appalled at the theft of my physical property and of my words. These were private letters. Not necessarily intimate or racy, but private. But maybe I'm just exercising an outmoded sense of ethical delicacy here.

Does anyone out there remember the distinction between public and private? Once upon a time, these were two separate, polar spheres of life. These words were actually antonyms. (Check the dictionary if you don't believe me.) Private was what happened in your bedroom, your closet or in your head, and it generally stayed there. Public was what you did, often in costume, if you thought anyone was watching. Everybody had private lives; only statesmen and royalty and movie stars had actual public lives. As recently as the 1970s, even these luminaries enjoyed some privacy, at least until they died; their drug taking, womanizing and sundry violations of the sodomy laws went largely unremarked unless they happened to crash the Mercedes into a tree as a result. Once the police got involved, things tended to become public. That was one of the rules, when there still were rules.

Of course, the border between public and private was always somewhat porous, compromised by the seepage of gossip. Gossip has always been with us. It's what makes us different from the invertebrates. But for the first million years or so of human evolution, gossip was an insider's game, a local affair. You had to be a member of court to know what the king was doing with his page.

Since roughly the moment that Gary Hart was caught stepping out of a town house with comely domestic-policy adviser Donna Rice, gossip has become the booming growth sector of journalistic enterprise. And the distinction between public and private has gradually—well, no, precipitously—disappeared. It took thousands of years to even develop the concept of privacy—the bedroom door, the billet-doux, that discreet hotel in Manhattan's East fifties where you paid in cash—and less than a generation to destroy it. Like mineral reserves that were once inaccessible to primitive technologies, the previously private amorous and pharmaceutical practices of celebrities, dead and living, have produced a bonanza for the fourth estate, even as the concept of celebrity has expanded to include approximately every third or fourth person.

The erosion of VIP privacy has been partly self-inflicted. Celebs in need of a career boost have learned to tell the story of their former drug, alcohol and/or sex addiction in exchange for a magazine cover shot. For those rare stars and pols who stubbornly cling to their privacy, there is usually a helpful chauffeur or maid willing to enlighten the rest of us about his or her employer's kinky foibles. The butler did it . . . or Charles's valet . . . or Diana's riding instructor.

Those lucky few Americans who are still neither rich nor famous—and without servants—far from rejoicing in their privacy, seem to be rushing to television studios to reveal the details of their private lives to the republic. This is not what Socrates meant when he said the unexamined life is not worth living. Like virginity in the '60s, privacy has become something to be gotten rid of—as soon as possible.

Blame Truman Capote, Donald Trump, Robin Leach or *People* magazine for contributing to this social breakdown, this mass attack of voyeurism/exhibitionism. But we're all a little guilty; don't say you never watched the O. J. Simpson trials. So herewith I offer a few practical tips for living in the era of glass houses:

> For those rare stars and pols who stubbornly cling to their privacy, there is usually a helpful chauffeur or maid willing to enlighten the rest of us about his or her employer's kinky foibles.

- When hiring domestic help, agree on your story in advance. It's ridiculously optimistic to think your personal assistant won't eventually try to sell the details of your life to a tabloid-TV show. So you should collaborate on what you would like revealed about yourself, and don't let the truth stand in your way. For instance, my assistant has promised to say that I was Michelle Pfeiffer's love slave.

- Burn your correspondence, shred your faxes, erase your E-mail.

- Since privacy has become such an undesirable commodity and exposure so valued, it occurs to me that crime would be considerably reduced if we deny publicity to all felony suspects and convicted criminals. No pictures except mug shots. And definitely no jailhouse interviews conducted by Diane Sawyer.

Which suggestion leads me back to my own recent brush with crime. How to deal with the creature who trafficked in my stolen correspondence? My first thought was to remove his (or her) fingernails with pliers. But that was hardly practical, no matter how desirable. My second thought was recourse to the law. My lawyers assured me I was on firm ground pursuing the case. They also mentioned, when pressed, what it might cost. Then there was the big negative factor: publicity. Did I really want to present the plagiarist with an opportunity to spread his own name and the name of his book all over the gossip columns? Wasn't it possible, even likely, that this was the very reason he had provoked me, in the hope of generating some cheap publicity?

If all this sounds far-fetched, I can only say that you don't know the phototropic individual in question. And you haven't paid close attention to the first part of this essay. In a world in which publicity and exposure—whether as a plagiarist or a pedophile—are seen as good fortune, perhaps the worst punishment we can devise is silence and anonymity.

On Accountability

by Ron Powers

ore than a decade ago, I moved with my wife and two sons from metropolitan New York City to Middlebury, Vermont. We'd nervously debated the opportunity for months. Did we dare sacrifice our city livelihoods for the uncertain rewards of teaching, writing and living in a small town filled with people we didn't know?

Our decision was sealed by an episode of, well, questionable manners one spring night behind Lincoln Center. In our haste to be on time for a chamber concert, we'd let down our guard and settled into a rare open parking spot on the street instead of crawling through the parking-garage labyrinth. While we were inside, someone—obviously eager to review the collection of audio cassettes on my dashboard—had elected not to wait until the conclusion of "Three Pieces in the Shape of a Pear" to ask my permission. Later, before we had picked out the last shard of glass from the floorboard nap, my wife, Honoree, and I had given our regards to Broadway—and to the whole complex urban-etiquette system of car-alarm sirens, extended middle fingers, snarling Akitas, Kryptonite locks, restraining orders, karate kicks and small-arms fire.

Today we find it hard to recall exactly what kind of behavior we expected to encounter in Vermont: more of the same, perhaps, but with better scenery and different accents. Okay, I'm pretty sure we didn't expect the same level of street crime. But as for callous behavior toward strangers (loud noise, littering, surliness in traffic and in stores and restaurants), the seedbed from which street crime darkly blossoms, we were likely on our urban guard. After all, we were not emigrating from the United States of America.

At a minimum, we braced for a long, chilly probation before admission into the Yankee town's insular society. What if we were shut out? What if American edginess just produced a different strain of menace here? What if we were exiting a scary novel by Don DeLillo only to enter one by Stephen King?

We could have saved ourselves the angst. Whatever we expected, what we got was a heady, almost mind-altering rush of civility. I still recall the near-illicit thrill that ran through us the first time we experimented with leaving our car doors unlocked downtown. Nothing happened! Yo! So we tried it again. And again. Out of our minds with uncut gemütlichkeit, we tried it with Honoree's purse lying on the front seat. It was still there when we got back. The earth moved!

Soon my New York–born wife—a gentle woman but nobody's fool when it comes to taking precautions—was exulting in this newfound absence of dread: telling the plumber to just go on in when he got there, the house was unlocked; even leaving signed blank checks on the kitchen table for the yardman.

But it was more than an absence of dread. It was an active presence of . . . something. We quickly relaxed into the pleasures of making our way through the town in the course of an ordinary day: wisecracking with Jack or Sean behind the counter at the post office. Lingering for a second cup of coffee and *The Times* at Blaney Blodgett's turn-of-the-century soda fountain, called Calvi's. Heading into Lazurus's dry-goods store to buy new shoes for the boys—and discovering that Helen had their sizes filed away in her memory from an earlier visit.

Our sons thrived on this presence. Ages six and four when we moved and now surging into young adulthood, they were profoundly children of the town. Kevin, the younger, relished waltzing into Steve's Park Diner on a Saturday morning and telling Barb, "I'll have the usual"—a bagel and cream cheese. Dean set records in the Middlebury pool and in the state with his medley-relay swimming teammates. Both are seasoned guitarists and community-theater actors. And both feel a fierce, almost curmudgeonly protectiveness for the permanence of this place. Walking past Amigo's Cantina with me one Saturday morning, aghast at a bright new coat of paint, Dean groused: "Before long we won't even be able to recognize this town!" His father's son.

One more important thing to know about accountability in a small town: It cuts both ways.

So what is this "presence" that confers such civility—and such richness of daily life—in a small town like Middlebury? It's nothing magical; no rite of initiation that makes people here any better than people anywhere else. Nor would I deny, if pressed, that burglaries do happen here, along with all the other failures of the human spirit—although with less frequency, intensity and, significantly, tolerance by the community at large.

The presence, I think, is accountability. It's not so much that people in small towns lack the inclination to misbehave; it's that we know how likely it is that we'll be held to account: not by the police, perhaps, but by people we know; people we face every day and will go on facing in the most personal and interconnected ways.

Cut me off in traffic and you're likely to be seated next to me tonight at the chamber of commerce banquet. Snarl at the waitress at Mr. Up's and she'll turn out to be your dentist's daughter. Go for those audio cassettes on the dashboard and, sure enough, someone will venture, "Land o' Goshen, Ethan! Isn't that the Powerses' car you're a-rummagin' in?" And so we work out modes of behavior to forestall these kinds of reckonings. We put our foot on the brake. Take time to kid around. Say please and thank you and isn't it a lovely day. Leave the damn tapes alone.

One more important thing to know about accountability in a small town: It cuts both ways. You don't just benefit from it as a newcomer. You're expected to provide your share. You give of yourself to the town. You serve on school boards, coach or umpire during the kids' baseball season and haul props for the Community Players. And the deeper your involvement goes, the more all those faces on the street distinguish themselves as you make your way through town. The easier it is to pass a pleasantry, aim a wisecrack. And the harder it is to imagine violating any of these faces, even with a rude gesture or remark. Those faces are part of you; part of your history. It's incredibly sophisticated, in its way. Trust me on that. I learned a few things about sophistication during my years in the city. Now, as a small-town guy, I'm learning a lot more.

Play Fair

by Heywood Hale Broun

Some years ago at a stop on the golf tour, Raymond Floyd deposited a drive in one of those tight little forests that exist to penalize the errant. After hitting his way out to a more advantageous lie, Floyd announced that while in the secrecy of the thicket, he had accidentally touched his golf ball, making him subject to a two-stroke penalty. Strokes can mean thousands of dollars, but Floyd waved off any praise for honesty, saying that if the world lived by the rules of the U.S. Golf Association, it might be a better place.

More than a half-century ago, when I became a sportswriter for a New York newspaper, I looked from the press box at a sea of men's fedoras. (It was leavened with the occasional headgear of a female who chose not to wait for the sexist, economically useful "ladies' day.") Much has changed in sports since then, and much of it for the better: Too many of the games of my youth excluded countless Americans because of race or ethnicity. But a distressing change has been the erosion of civility among both players and spectators. We've traveled far from the hatted crowd—which rooted for the home team but applauded good play by both sides—to that of today's angry thousands, thousands who a few years ago in Philadelphia cheered a life-threatening injury to football star Michael Irvin.

In the years when I was a sports correspondent for CBS, I tried as much as authority allowed to chronicle the games played for the sheer joy of the playing—things like golf tournaments on frozen lakes (red golf balls and sleds carrying coffee and grog). I wasn't trying to be cute in these bypath trips; I was trying to celebrate the true meaning of sports.

Small children, finding the adult world both large and unfair, take refuge in the certainty of games in which, by consent, they make up and abide by a set of regulations. Watch a group of youngsters improvising something with a stick and a ball, and see what happens when a player makes an unwelcome move.

"You can't do that! It's against the rules!" will come piping cries.

It was in this spirit, which nowadays seems more than a bit naive, that Grantland Rice wrote, "When the One Great Scorer comes to write against your name, he marks not that you won or lost—but how you played the game."

Years later I tried to tell Brooklyn Dodger manager Leo Durocher about a rookie pitcher's terrific B-squad performance. "Never mind how good he was," barked Leo, "just tell me if he won." He was only a little ahead of the modern maxim "Winning isn't everything, it's the only thing." This obviously means that if you can get away with breaking the rules, you do. At that point, of course, sport ceases to be a well-structured sanctuary from The Great Game of Life.

> Small children, finding the adult world both large and unfair, take refuge in the certainty of games in which, by consent, they make up and abide by a set of regulations.

Ironically, the man most associated with the idea that winning is the only thing, Vince Lombardi, was as devoted to rules as any group of children in a made-up game. He wanted his Green Bay Packers to play fiercely but fairly. I remember an occasion when, on the way to a game, his team suffered a light blackout while dressing. My camera crew provided battery lamps to permit orderly preparation. Later, at a championship game in Florida, Lombardi banned the press from workouts but was confronted by, among others, my producer, our camera crew and me. He came to a halt and snarled: "Oh, it's you guys. I owe you. You've got ten minutes." The voice was harsh, but it spoke the words of civil obligation.

One of the factors that contribute to today's desperation of competition—with its concomitant incivility—is the notion put forth by many coaches that winners have better character than losers. Paradoxically, this often changes a genial pair of players into a couple of thugs slanging each other in the fight for character. The cry of "Good shot!" lies buried in the vicar's garden where tennis, once the most genteel of sports, had its beginnings. Of course, all such gentlemanly cries may stick in the throat when the shot has cost the loser a very large sum of money. The business of sporting rewards—which makes millionaires of the mediocre—has added a greed factor to gridirons and golf courses. Fun and games have become fun, high stakes and games. Deplorable behavior comes in the door when dollars fly out the window.

For some years, groups of Wall Street whiz kids would take a keg of beer and a bunch of rugby shirts to Staten Island. If Bank X had only thirteen players, Brokerage House Y would lend them a couple. The main idea was to get rid of frustration with a bump-bang morning. Perhaps such games still take place, but many more of the financial and business community's part-time athletes are now in basketball leagues where standings are carefully kept. It's believed by these players that successful play can take one out of the mailroom and up to accounts receivable, a first step to the board-room. So it's not surprising that elbow-in-the-mouth play occurs.

Maybe nobody you know has stooped to these levels. Yet there is no denying that the great decline in player and spectator deco-rum cuts a pretty wide swath. Have you noticed that when the fights inevitably break out at a hockey game virtually every fan roars his (or her) support for a favorite Tyson on ice? So far, golf and ten-nis crowds mostly refrain from shouting at critical moments, but umpires and marshals increasingly must shush partisanship on the edge of disruption. A pity when one thinks that even in the wildest days of the Jazz Age, football crowds contented themselves with the singing of derisive songs about John Harvard, Eli Yale, et al.

Of course, to old geezers like me, the golden age is always somewhere back down the road. But while I don't think we're on our way to doom, I do, like all would-be sages, have some advice for anyone interested in preserving the notion of sportsmanship: Focus less on the score and more on our heroes. As we admired the magic of Michael Jordan, a grace beyond comprehension, let us admire the muscular ballet of the tennis-playing Williams sisters; the good-guy image of quarterback Peyton Manning, son of Archie and proof that heroes' children can also be heroes; and all the men and women whose accomplishments—win or lose—make us feel that we've seen legends alive.

When Samuel Johnson compiled the first great dictionary of the English language, he also expressed a philosophy. Sport was defined as "Play; Diversion; Game; Frolic and Tumultuous Merriment." Something, therefore, outside the cares and chaos of daily life.

Not for nothing was Johnson's century called the Age of Reason.

The Etiquette of E-Mail
by Owen Edwards

tiquette is always at its most tenuous on the untamed edges of frontiers. People may want to mind their manners, but figuring out those manners can be very tricky. In the Wild West of cyberspace, no innovation is in need of civilizing more than electronic mail, a.k.a. E-mail. Taming this frontier matters, because whether we like it or not, E-mail is here to stay.

Those who've yet to embrace it might just as well give in, because, though far from perfect, E-mail is irresistibly useful. It fills a niche between the immediacy of the telephone and the deliberation of the letter, combining electronic speed and convenience with the permanence of the printed word. That makes E-mail a medium for clipped business memos and mass-distributed jokes, as well as more literate repartee. I use the word literate advisedly, considering the acceptance among young Netter writers of such cyber terms as "convo" for conversation and "brb" for be right back. Yes, E-mail is a strange hybrid, like the mythical creature Woody Allen once described as having the head of a lion and the body of a lion, but not the same lion. As such, the old rules of communicating don't always apply, and a few new ones—what some have dubbed "Netiquette"—ought to be considered.

A few years ago I carried on an active E-mail correspondence with a Silicon Valley billionaire, a man in part responsible for the growth of E-mail itself. He and I were collaborating on a book, but years from now, should anyone read our missives—if you can call them that—he may wonder if the two of us were using the same medium. I tend to construct my notes with a salutation, a few sociable lines to ease into the serious stuff at hand and a personal sign-off. In contrast, my collaborator's responses are simply my notes sent back to me with his comments inserted. No salutation, no small talk, no sign-off. Of course, this is business communication, even if the business is literary. Still, much of Voltaire's voluminous correspondence had to do with work, too, and remains an elegant link to the great letter-writing traditions of the Enlightenment.

My correspondent, who's been using E-mail for many years as an Internet entrepreneur as well as an academic, has obviously outgrown any romantic attachment to the medium. Conversely, I think of it as instantly delivered letters in which the politesse of both personal and business correspondence applies—and cling optimistically to the belief that E-mail will revive the diminished art of letter writing. But my views and those of my coauthor both have validity, which means that there's a wide range of acceptable approaches; his may be terse, but it's efficient. Efficiency, after all, is the whole point of E-mail. Still, I hope I will be forgiven for pushing my own epistolary agenda: bringing a little decorum to what can be a rather fast-and-loose process.

E-mail is a strange hybrid, like the mythical creature Woody Allen once described as having the head of a lion and the body of a lion, but not the same lion.

Sometimes when I read my collaborator's self-styled replies, it helps to consider E-mail's origins. It was developed in 1969 by a Defense Department agency as a means of connecting various computer networks. Its no-nonsense character sprang from those pragmatic roots.

Today, as E-mail grows and changes by the minute, no attempt to train or restrain it can meet with complete success. But with just a bit of patience, the "mail" in E-mail can be a grace note that makes the form elegant as well as electronic. For starters, if, as you type an E-mail message, you think of yourself with pen in hand and a sheet of fine white paper on the desk, you might balance convenience with care. There are times, though, when only ink on paper will do. For wedding invitations, anniversaries and other relatively formal events, E-mail just doesn't seem proper. For impromptu dinner parties, however, it's a boon. Thank-you notes are still more meaningful in real rather than virtual form, but electronic gratitude is better than no gratitude at all.

Internet providers are making E-mail easier to send all the time. You can, as frequent users know, pick up entire newspaper articles or congressional transcripts from Web sites, drop them into an E-mail "envelope" and whisk them to your two-hundred closest "pen" pals. But on the receiving end, your convenience may be someone else's headache. Hardly anyone likes to do a lot of reading on the screen, so cut out the article and stick it in a real envelope. Or use that quaint old technology, the fax.

On principle, I have taken to deleting jokes unread whenever they're E-mailed to someone's entire address book. Before E-mail, no one ever would have licked fifty envelopes to pass along a page of dubious humor to friends and acquaintances. But here the ease of E-mail works both ways: If jokes require no effort to send, they also require no effort to toss out.

Among the most blunt features of this blunt medium is "reply," which allows you to simply stick an answer onto the original message. With the option of that instantaneous response, there's no point expecting people to go the slower route of clicking onto a new page. Some of us may prefer the waltz, but, as the song goes, rock 'n' roll is here to stay.

Several years ago, before I succumbed to E-mail's lure, the writer Stewart Brand, the visionary behind the *Whole Earth Catalog*, told me he found E-mail to be one of the most intimate methods of communicating he'd ever experienced. I doubted him at the time, but after two years of electronic correspondence I understand what he meant. Today I make consistent contact with far more relatives and friends than ever before, often in a more thoughtful way than the telephone allows. I've noticed that my determination to think of most E-mail as letters and notes has meant that I elicit largely literate responses. And I've realized that I'm more flexible with the new medium than with words on paper. It's been said that first we shape our inventions but eventually they shape us. That may be true, but as we adapt to the new, we can still observe good form.

E-mail veterans like my Silicon Valley collaborator contend there's no point in putting any literary effort, never mind proper spelling, into Internet exchanges. After all, they argue, most recipients just hit delete and the message vanishes. But that's like saying it's pointless to use good grammar on the phone, since the conversation fades away as it takes place. Words, like music, reverberate in the mind, and, as Enzo Ferrari proved, elegance and speed are not incompatible.

The Sound and My Fury
•. by William Norwich .•——

"Please, be quiet." That's the first line of my second novel. The working title is The Passing of Mrs. Astorbilt. Based on no living person, I swear, the amalgamated name is meant only to personify the genteel spirit once found in New York. My aging Mrs. Astorbilt is bankrupt, her hair no longer in curl. In the sound and fury of the city, she is drowning. "Please, be quiet," Mrs. Astorbilt entreats, begging for release from the noise made by usurpers screaming to mark their new New York territory.

As for the remainder of my novel, well, ask my neighbors when it can be written. My New York apartment faces a courtyard on the Upper East Side. Starting at 7 A.M., Monday through Saturday, there is construction and renovation on three sides. Then there's the family of the famous pit-bull lawyer that fights and screams and locks its barking dog out for hours.

If status can be measured in part by how much space you take up, then noise—from private jets to boom boxes—is an indisputable form of aural land grabbing, the Hoovering-up of serenity that, like a public park, once belonged to everyone. And if you think the world is noisier than ever, you're not hearing things. Just ask Bill Clinton—oh, and speak up when you do. It's no accident that a former president had to resort to a hearing aid at such a relatively young age. After all, he presided over the country Oscar Wilde once called "the noisiest that ever existed." As if to make Wilde's point, the Environmental Protection Agency gave up and closed its noise-control department in 1982.

At Flents Products, the Norwalk, Connecticut, concern that has been making earplugs since 1927, business has been increasing by about 30 percent annually in recent years, the company reports. "What? What did you say?" joked interior decorator Mario Buatta when queried about the latest noise levels. "There's no end to it. New York is a city that's never going to be finished—and the noise at parties, when the band plays so loudly . . ."

Noise can be defined as any sound you don't want to hear—and it's not just a Manhattan malady. Aspen has restricted the loudest takeoffs and landings of the rich and famous at hours when good folks are asleep. And one community in the Hamptons, the summer-resort enclave on New York's Long Island, is said to have purchased a sound meter to help in enforcing noise limits in the velvet burg. *New York Times* columnist Russell Baker wrote that high noise levels come about as a result of "society's determination to entertain you whether you like it or not": Muzak in elevators, automated voices on telephone calls, the decibel levels in trendy restaurants, snowmobiles and jet skis, the sounds that spill from stereo headsets, the blasting radios from other cars. And why is it they only mow lawns at posh resorts on Saturday mornings, when guests would like to sleep in? By comparison, the whoops expected on New Year's Eve seem rather quaint.

Are we addicted to noise? As psychologist and lawyer Rex Julian Beaber told the *Los Angeles Times*, "Consciousness abhors a vacuum." We dread silence and fill in the gaps with the din of cellular phones, computer games, whatever. But Beaber's point goes further. He compared the mind's appetite for stimulation to the body's need for food: The brain has gotten so used to audio stimulation, it craves noise, making it a substance we abuse like other stimulants, such as coffee, sugar, alcohol or even rock 'n' roll.

Is the solution to just say no to noise? On a personal level, yes, sure: Enter noise-rehab immediately! But on a more serious (and quieter) note, combating noise is no easy task. You might just as well stand naked in the middle of Times Square with a sign reading "I'm no fun" when you ask someone to be quiet. An endless era of Manifest Self-Actualization is one of the more pernicious legacies of those hedonistic 1960s. We are a culture of narcissists, not neighbors. It may be brave, even noble, but it just isn't cool to ask people to quiet themselves. Noise and other expressions of bad manners occur, said sociologist Bryan Wilson, because fellow citizens "are no longer seen to deserve treatment as dignified equals."

> Noise and other expressions of bad manners occur, said sociologist Bryan Wilson, because fellow citizens "are no longer seen to deserve treatment as dignified equals."

That parents might raise quiet children is one hope. But overworked moms and dads assuage their guilt by indulging their young with ever-increasing and often noisy toys and games.

I suppose we'll all have to become soldiers for silence. Warning: There will be slings and arrows. But sometimes civility will prevail. A few years ago, a certain Mrs. Willinghelper (a fictional moniker) was giving a luncheon at her Fifth Avenue apartment for board members of one of her charities. When the rumbling from construction on a nearby town house threatened to ruin the afternoon, she called the owner of the house, who lived in Europe. He gallantly ordered work stopped for an hour, during which Mrs. Willinghelper and her guests could enjoy their meal and conversation.

"I'd like to try something like that in the movie theater when someone is talking," says Mario Buatta, "but I'm afraid of what he'd say, or worse, do."

Rita Kip, whose family lived in Manhattan when it was called New Amsterdam, once tried asking people at the next table in a Nantucket restaurant to quiet down. "It wasn't a happy experience," reported Kip, who forsook a fashionably blasé stance for a more assertive one. "They were horrified, looked at me as if I were from outer space and did not lower their voices."

"I tried asking someone to be quiet at The Ashram," the California spa, a fashion-editor friend told me. "We were on a meditative walk in the hills and this Chatty Cathy wouldn't stop. Very politely I told her I needed some silence. She said she understood but then proceeded to explain how she had a problem with not being able to stop talking! I just walked away."

I have had mixed results myself when asking for quiet. When I telephoned the patriarch of the household with the barking dog, requesting a reprieve while on a particularly painful deadline, he responded: "F— you! If you don't like noise, don't live in New York."

Another neighbor did oblige when I begged him to curtail his son's drum playing. Now their town house has been sold and its renovations roar each morning. Fortunately, though, after the jackhammers are stayed, the house, I'm told, will become a center for cosmetic surgery. Not a likely setting for loud parties, I have to assume.

Rekindling the Holiday Spirit

· by Sally Quinn ·

I'm dreaming of a white Candlemas. Snow on the ground, crisp, cold weather, a welcoming fire roaring in the hearth, candles flickering on every table, tall branches of flowering quince in pretty vases, a big pot of delicious stew, warm, crusty bread, a bottle of robust red wine, some good friends . . .

The Christmas holidays, with all the hyperactivity and forced frivolity they engender, couldn't contrast more in tone with my favorite holiday: Candlemas, February 2. This religious celebration has come to symbolize the advent of spring amid winter's lingering darkness. It's observed by filling the house with candles and fires, as well as flowers, to proclaim the start of new life and hope. I look forward to the tranquillity of Candlemas as I toil my way through the frenzy of the Christmas season.

Oh, am I dreaming of a white Candlemas! No questionably appropriate gifts to give or receive, no wrapping of packages or running out of paper, ribbon or tags. No Christmas cards or mimeographed family updates. No eating and drinking too much. No chilly exchanges with husbands over the holidays' uneven division of labor. No perfect hostesses showing me up and making me feel guilty. No trying to please everyone: mince pies for Jane, oyster dressing for Suzy and ambrosia for Harry. No returning gifts and endlessly writing thank-you notes—or bribing the children to get them to write theirs. I'm exhausted just thinking about it all.

It's a cliché to say that something has gone haywire with

Christmas, that the commercial aspects of the holiday have overwhelmed its spiritual and social meaning. But things are getting out of hand. It's not just that it's become so tied up in materialism that you feel on some level that you and your family are simply dupes of clever marketing strategies. It is that the sense of generosity of spirit, of caring about other people and their feelings, seems to be disappearing as well.

Sadly, I've found that the stress of Christmas often brings out the worst in people rather than the best. It's almost as if they wait a whole year to misbehave: There's the uncle who becomes intoxicated at Christmas dinner and falls into his soup, embarrassing everyone; the "friend" who presents you with a bathing suit you couldn't possibly fit into; the spouse who gives you something practical instead of the pearl earrings you've been hinting at all year; the boss who sends you a ham when he knows perfectly well you're a vegetarian.

Some friends and I got together several years ago for a Christmas support group. We held it at the cocktail hour, so we were well fortified by the end. It was great. We got out all of our hostility and dove back into the fray with renewed gusto after just one session—and a large dose of mutual sympathy and shared advice.

As a longtime chronicler and observer of Washington's social scene and author of *The Party: A Guide to Adventurous Entertaining,*

I have a few ideas about the ways we handle certain communal occasions. It is in the spirit of the season that I offer some suggestions on how we might make the holidays a bit more civilized.

- The biggest and most important piece of advice is to scale things down. Just because Gogo Gotrocks always throws the perfect party and gives everyone there a personalized present beautifully wrapped, it doesn't mean you have to.

- If you don't have to, don't give parties at all over the holidays. Wait until, say, Candlemas or Valentine's Day, when it's so dreary and we don't have quite so many things to do. (Who couldn't do with one less commitment in December?)

- Make an agreement with your adult siblings and cousins to buy gifts only for the children. Then if you can't stand it, pick numbers out of a hat and let each person buy one present for just one member of the family.

- If possible, pick one good store and try buying everything there. It really saves time, and you can get almost all of your shopping done in a few hours.

- If you think teenagers or struggling young adults with little kids would rather have cash, give it to them. It'll be easier on you, and they'll appreciate it more than something that might be relegated to a closet shelf.

- Make a pact with your closest friends to forgo presents until another time, when you see something you think they might truly like. That's a good way to keep the holiday spirit in the air year-round.

- Don't overdo decorations. Besides the tree, settle for a simple wreath, some holly, a few well-placed poinsettias and swags of evergreen. (It's Christmas, not Mardi Gras.)

- Rethink Christmas cards. Most people are in regular contact by phone or fax or E-mail, so cards are no longer the means of communication they once were. Besides, many people simply open them and toss them into a basket or throw them away.
- Have Christmas dinner late in the day. That will give you time to open presents, oversee the meal, get dressed, and still relax and enjoy yourself before collapsing into bed.
- Share holiday dinners with another family, so that you're not playing host every year. Changing the dinner-party mix also could bring some new sparkle to a predictable feast: Your Aunt Gertrude may look pretty swell seated beside their cousin Horace.
- Consider doing something that invokes the true meaning of the season—for example, offer to make sandwiches at a shelter for the homeless—to remind you that there actually is a point to the holidays.

Smugly American
by Andrew Nagorski

e were having lunch at Nino's, very much the kind of restaurant near the Piazza di Spagna in Rome that I thought the couple visiting from the U.S. would enjoy. As we tucked into our luscious pasta mista, the wife stiffened, looked angrily around and announced with alarm, "Someone is smoking a cigar." Her husband tried assuring her that he didn't smell anything, but it was too late: She'd spied the culprit on the other side of the packed restaurant.

"He's so far away, dear," her frustrated spouse implored. "Let it be."

"Either he puts out his cigar or I'm leaving," she declared, pushing back her chair.

He turned to me in abject desperation. "Andy," he pleaded, "could you do something?"

What I wanted to do was hide under the table. Instead, I reluctantly made my way over to the smoker. A Roman god must have intervened, because the cigar lover turned out to be an American. As such, he was unfazed by my mumbling, apologetic request, and—miracle of miracles—complied immediately. "I'm used to this in the States," he said, laughing.

But this was Rome, where smoking a cigar in a restaurant is hardly a capital offense. Don't get me wrong: I don't smoke, and I don't appreciate being surrounded by people who do. Nonetheless, during my many years of roaming the world as a foreign correspondent for *Newsweek*, I have tried, within reasonable limits, to adapt to local customs. Simple manners dictate the need for a bit of deference to your hosts, and the farther from home one travels, the more important the basic social graces become. (If a New Yorker can easily give unwitting offense in rural Mississippi, an American tourist can certainly stir outright resentment in an Egyptian village.)

Deference doesn't mean abandoning basic beliefs or allowing anyone to mistreat you; it does mean acknowledging that American concepts of etiquette are far from universally accepted or even understood. Like certain wines, some homegrown attitudes just don't travel well. One of them is political correctness, particularly as it relates to smoking, diet and interaction between the sexes.

> Deference doesn't mean abandoning basic beliefs or allowing anyone to mistreat you; it does mean acknowledging that American concepts of etiquette are far from universally accepted or even understood.

In the 1950s, many Americans strutted into foreign countries, flush with the might of their new superpower status and convinced that they had everything to teach and nothing to learn. This brand of traveler was quickly dubbed The Ugly American. His primary characteristic: a total insensitivity to local customs and etiquette. The timbre of the 1960s helped soften his harsh image. This change in attitude was symbolized by the newly formed Peace Corps, with its brigades of idealistic volunteers in search of a "meaningful cultural experience." With the upsurge in global travel since the '60s, more and more Americans have learned how much richer a trip can be when they stay attuned to the local sensibilities.

Still, I worry that a new negative stereotype may be developing around the world: The P.C. American. This hubristic breed shares many of the smug assumptions of cultural superiority that characterized The Ugly American, but its behavioral patterns are radically different. Instead of drinking, smoking and traveling the global village intent on having a good time at the expense of propriety, these partisans of political correctness can be fastidious eaters and drinkers (if they drink at all), borderline fanatics about health fads or humorless dogmatists when it comes to gender roles.

The perception of them—and, by extension, of all Americans—is fostered as much by media images as it is by first-hand encounters. From across the Atlantic or Pacific, the U.S. can look like a rather strange country. Consider a land where six-year-olds can be accused of sexual harassment, where complimenting a woman on her looks is akin to courting professional disaster, where smokers have the social status of child molesters, where people compulsively talk about cutting down on fat and cholesterol while gorging themselves on junk food.

Many American travelers quickly give the lie to this one-dimensional picture. But a small band of them loaded down with P.C. baggage can reinforce it. During the war in Afghanistan in the 1980s, Western aid workers and journalists flooded into the Pakistani border town of Peshawar. Soon a bitter dispute erupted among the American women. Some of them wore the shalwar kameez, which consists of baggy pants and a loose tunic. This was a reasonable concession to local sensibilities, nothing like the extensive head covering required by such stridently Muslim countries as Iran. Yet the other American women berated them for "giving in to the mullahs."

The disproportionate power of a few to shape the way in which an entire country is perceived is at its worst when travelers like my dinner guest in Rome overreact to a violation of their personal P.C. code. They're ready to take up arms, for example, when someone lights up in a "no smoking" area, the rule rather than the exception in French restaurants. Aside from raising the profile of the P.C. American, such rigidity can guarantee joyless travels. People who are endlessly agitated about the lack of vegetarian dishes on a Hungarian menu, or who try to figure out the MSG content of a Chinese meal, will hardly savor their dinner. And women in a constant state of alert over often boorish but usually harmless feats of misplaced machismo may find Italy and any Latin American country more of an ordeal than a delight.

Of course, there are Americans who go overboard to impress others with their willingness to adapt to local customs. At a dinner in Taipei hosted by a local tycoon, an American businessman kept trying to demonstrate his love for all things Taiwanese. When the pigeon course arrived, he snagged the bird's head with his chopsticks and crunched away. His host nodded politely, but his real reaction, I suspect, was one of puzzlement at such an obsequious show of deference.

Foreigners are particularly baffled by tales from America's gender wars. At our dinner table in Moscow during my Russian posting, I recall with only partial amusement the question raised by a Polish guest after she'd heard "battlefield" accounts from some American visitors: "How do you reproduce?" That level of incredulity can also be seen in Tokyo, where U.S.-bound businessmen are taught about avoiding sexual-harassment suits. Pragmatism aside, the prevailing view in Japan is that Americans have gone slightly crazy. The French would amend that characterization to *complètement fou*.

Tweaking Americans for their dogmatism has almost become a popular sport overseas. A Russian biologist I know gleefully recalls a conversation she had with a group of very P.C. American scientists at the time of the Clarence Thomas hearings regarding his Supreme Court appointment. One of the Americans asked her if she could imagine a male boss making suggestive remarks to a female subordinate in a Russian office. Absolutely, she responded. "And what would be the reaction of the other women in the office?" he asked. Her reply: "They'd be jealous." The Americans retreated into stunned silence.

Admittedly, the cultural divide on some issues can be enormous. But indignation, not to mention dining on ornithological extremities, is hardly the sensible reaction. A bit of reasoned discussion illuminating the U.S. zeitgeist might help. So might a bit of lightening up by Americans, who should acknowledge that there can be very different standards of judging what is socially acceptable. A compliment for la bella signora and a little smoke circling lazily above a distant table are hardly grounds for an international incident. At the very least, they shouldn't prevent you from relishing your pasta mista.

The Right of Way

by Owen Edwards

uring a brief, rather dreary period in my life, I lived and worked in Los Angeles. (The fault was in myself, not in Hollywood's stars.) As anyone who's ever visited that sprawling city knows, the automobile is the shared communal experience, the great, unavoidable leveler. Whether you're luxuriating in a Bentley or making do in a battered Dodge van, drive you must. Everywhere. All the time.

Thus, one of L.A.'s standard laments: With everyone locked in his or her car, you can never get to know anybody. My impression was quite the opposite. As a captive on such raging concrete rivers as the Santa Monica and San Diego freeways, I got to know people all too well through their behavior behind the wheel. At least, I got to know them well enough to be certain I didn't want to know them any better. Aggressive, inconsiderate, angry and arrogant, many of my fellow drivers were doltish, dangerous or both. I could easily picture them cutting in line at the movies, reaching in front of me at the table, dominating a conversation or breezing through a door I had held open for someone else. Perhaps, in some rare instance, someone can be rude on the road but otherwise courteous in life. But do you really think you could spend a pleasant evening with the motorized menace who absolutely refuses to observe the simple etiquette of the two-lane merge? Generally, I'm convinced, the way people behave on four wheels is a tip-off to their behavior in social situations. In short, we are as we drive.

My father, a decorous man with an aura of the Victorian era clinging to him, was my driving teacher. He constantly emphasized that beneath all the traffic laws and unwritten rules of the road, the quality that defines good driving is grace. "If you do things gracefully," he would say as we swept down New Jersey's Garden State Parkway in his big Buick Roadmaster, "you'll cut down on the chances for unpleasant surprises."

> On the road, as in life, impeccable behavior, like other virtues, must often be its own reward.

A former college football player who liked nothing better than to go out dancing with my mother, Dad saw the highway as he might have seen a crowded dance floor, where a combination of grace and its handmaiden, courtesy, is essential to keep from throwing yourself and everyone else off stride. You need to know not only where other dancers are at the moment but where they will be when you are alongside them. As he danced, so he drove. And despite a tendency to go too fast and suffer fools ungladly, Dad had a long, safe life on the road.

If you single out the attributes of a truly well-mannered person—attentiveness, unselfishness, anticipation, exquisite timing, a concern for the smooth working of the social contract and a certain degree of pride in understanding all levels of the game—you will also be listing the virtues of a good driver. Take the elegant character who, at a party, senses from across the room that a conversation is lagging and manages to get there in time to inject new life without having the welcome intervention seem at all contrived. Count on this to be the person who will spot, just ahead on the road, someone about to be forced out of a lane by an oblivious driver's clumsiness and will slow down or move over to create a space.

Then there's the kind of person who finds herself at dinner seated beside a combative ideologue but, by finding a way to create a cordial bridge between opposing viewpoints, diffuses the harangue. She will also see in the rearview mirror a speeding driver rapidly approaching in her lane and, rather than make a race of it or force her slower speed on the other car, will cede the lane without a competitive thought.

Just as there are countless parallels between good form on the road and good form in society, there are plenty of unhappy links between bad driving and bad manners. The core of rudeness on the road is the same as that at the heart of all boorishness: the pernicious little idea that no one else on earth matters quite so much as oneself. Some people seem convinced that there's a constitutionally guaranteed right of way that applies to them above all others. You can see this in the person who walks ahead of you through a door and lets it close in your face and in the driver who pulls in front of you without a signal or even a look. Call such lapses absentmindedness if you like, but when someone doesn't care to notice what's going on around him, what we have is egocentricity at work.

The incessant talker ready to turn a simple conversation about the weather into a major debate must certainly be the same person who would much rather use the horn than the brakes. Is it any surprise that the noisiest streets this side of Cairo are in my old hometown, New York, a city infamous for its argumentative denizens? By contrast, in the high-couth city of San Francisco (my current hometown), it's hard to get a disagreement going about anything. And, not coincidentally, the sound of a car horn in the City by the Bay is greeted with horror by drivers and pedestrians alike.

The surest gauge of driver civility, especially on the West Coast, is the four-way stop. If decorum on the highway is akin to a waltz, the proper working of the four-way stop is closer to the intricacies of the minuet. There are rules, of course: First in/first through, the driver to the right has the honors, etc. But what's really required is a complete willingness to let others go first.

On the road, as in life, impeccable behavior, like other virtues, must often be its own reward. Certainly, rude drivers tend to think of their mannerly brethren as chumps and losers. Such is the irony of an uncouth world. Even entirely decent drivers may take for granted the good deeds of four-wheeled chivalry. And to be honest, you and I may sometimes be tempted to give in to the desire to retaliate: to slow down in front of that annoying horn blower, to block the passage of the lane weaver who cannot be bothered to signal and, in other ways, just this once, to balance the scales of justice. My advice is to resist these impulses. Who holds the door for whom and whether a political argument spoils a dinner party are important matters, but not life-or-death questions. But a highway on which everyone subscribes to a Lord of the Flies ethic can only become more dangerous than it already is. So ease up, let the bounders misbehave, and bask in the superiority of your amazing grace.

II
LITTLE THINGS
MEAN A LOT

If you think those small acts of kindness go unnoticed,
think again.

On Being a Gentleman
by David Brown

nita Loos claimed that gentlemen prefer blondes but marry brunettes. Cole Porter said, "Most gentlemen don't like love/They just like to kick it around." And George Bernard Shaw added an androgynous note when he defined a gentleman as "a man, more often a woman, who owes nothing and leaves the world in debt to him."

Times have changed, as Cole Porter also said, but standards of gentlemanly behavior have not. Such behavior is as cool and hip today as it ever was. In fact, one of the best examples of it I can recall took place some four decades ago. Back then, the first mezzanine of New York's art deco Radio City Music Hall was reserved for A-list power figures. They were escorted aloft from a walnut-paneled VIP lounge by way of an elevator the size of a phone booth. It was operated by an equally diminutive pageboy. On one occasion, the pageboy's lone passenger put out his hand in greeting and said, "Hello. I'm Dwight D. Eisenhower." Whether a former president or a plain old citizen, a gentleman does not assume he is recognized on sight—as true now as ever.

There are times, however, when he does not wish to be identified. Cary Grant, seated beside a dowager at a Park Avenue dinner party, was asked, "And what is it you do, Mr. Grant?" (That in itself was a social no-no.) The mega–movie star, unwilling to inflict the pain of a gaffe on his questioner, replied, "Oh, I'm in the perfume business." It was true, although his role as a board member of Fabergé was not the one for which he was famous.

Cary Grant notwithstanding, gentlemen do not always come clothed in formal dress or, these days, Armani. They often wear blue collars. I have observed more politeness on Hollywood sound stages or construction sites than in some boardrooms or fashionable restaurants.

How, then, does one make the cut? Here are my rules:

- Never be rude, regardless of provocation. This will infuriate the provoker, who gets off on bleats of wounded feelings.
- Always acknowledge a gift, be it something in a blue Tiffany box or a single yellow rose from your corner vendor.
- Dress within reason (no black tie in the jungle), according to the inner man—your own true self. I wore a green fedora, tie and jacket all through my undergraduate years at Stanford. I dress conservatively even on movie sets, as did Alfred Hitchcock, because *c'est moi*. Don't be intimidated by the reigning dress code.
- Speak softly.
- Say "please" and "thank you," words that Andy Rooney believes have nearly dropped out of the language.
- Avoid a stuffy, patronizing demeanor, although if you have one, you'll probably have to be exorcised to lose it. Today's gentleman may be daring in conversation but always respectful of unpopular opinion. He may be fearless about taking a contrarian stand

> Cary Grant notwithstanding, gentlemen do not always come clothed in formal dress or, these days, Armani. They often wear blue collars.

but will never do so in an abrasive way. Above all, he does not put his listeners to sleep.

- Do not talk or eat with your hands.
- Treat everyone the same. A gentleman makes no distinction among classes. As Professor Higgins said in defense of his dealings with Eliza Doolittle in *My Fair Lady*: "It's not as though I treat you differently from anyone else. I treat you the same."
- Keep your word, especially if you've made a bad bargain.
- Return telephone calls the same day (except those from argumentative callers), and reply to all but pest letters. (Show-business types tend to be especially delinquent in this department.)
- Be unconcerned about taking credit, yet give it freely even to those who are undeserving but need it.
- View the world with wit and laughter: Without a robust sense of humor, a fellow is a dope who doesn't know the score.
- Never reveal your worth to anyone but your accountant and, depending on the state of your marriage, your spouse. Braggarts are boors, especially those who talk about money. Romantic dalliances (they used to be called "conquests" before feminists got us thinking) are also off conversational limits. Always send flowers after a night of passion, and don't steal away once you are sated. As La Rochefoucauld said: "A gentleman may love like a lunatic but not like a beast." Don't be beastly.
- Never tell truth that hurts unless it hurts only you. John Henry Newman got it right when he wrote, "It is almost a definition of a gentleman to say that he is the one who never inflicts pain."
- Be more interested in doing right than in being right.

Happily, I know a lot of men who observe these rules. Jack Nicholson, his bad-boy image aside, almost always does; so does Paul Newman (unless you ask for his autograph, which he considers foolish); Tom Hanks is as admirable as the characters he usually plays; Morgan Freeman is the very definition of a gentleman in dress and deportment; and Clint Eastwood will make your day with his manners and modesty. Cary Grant and Gary Cooper were true models in their day. Gentlewomen include Barbara Walters, Diane Sawyer, Sherry Lansing and, in their time, Audrey Hepburn and Claudette Colbert.

Inasmuch as I value women's opinions on this subject, my secretary and my wife demand to be heard. My secretary, Doris Wood, offers this definition: "A gentleman is able to express himself with a vocabulary larger than four-letter words." And Helen Gurley Brown's unpredictable take: "A gentleman puts up with your use of four-letter words but uses none of his own—except in bed." Go figure.

I prefer Samuel Butler's reverie about gentlemen:. "If we are asked what is the most essential characteristic that underlies this word, the word itself will guide us to gentleness, absence of browbeating or overbearing manners, absence of fuss, and generally consideration for the other people."

Don't Forget the Flowers

by Cokie Roberts and Steven V. Roberts

We have a deal about flowers. Steve plants them, weeds them and keeps them watered; Cokie picks them, arranges them and places them around the house. We have a similar deal about vegetables. Steve grows; Cokie cooks. Then we try to say: "How pretty...good idea...lovely pansies...great peppers." And the simplest phrase of all: "Thank you." For what you just did. And for everything else.

We both love living with flowers, but they also symbolize a larger point. The smallest gestures, repeated over a lifetime together, acquire enormous meaning. That's why you should never take each other for granted. Every day, find a way to say, "I love you. I want to make you happy."

Of course, big gifts play an important role in any good marriage; they're a way of marking significant dates and events. For one anniversary, Cokie bought Steve season tickets to the Redskins' games, even though that meant he'd be gone for eight Sundays every fall. For his part, Steve has long followed the old saw, If God wanted women to get electrical appliances for their birthdays, He would not have invented jewelry stores. But in the end, the tiny tokens of affection matter even more. We were reminded of their importance while collaborating on our book, *From This Day Forward*.

After more than thirty years of marriage, we've learned at least:

to listen to each other and understand each other's tastes and habits. If Cokie is cooking pasta and Steve will be working at home the next day, she'll add extra for his lunch. If Steve's grilling fish, he'll take Cokie's piece off first. (She likes it barely warm.) She'll buy the spicy Tabasco mayonnaise he likes to spread on sandwiches. He'll set the table the way she prefers, with napkins that match the plates and glasses. (That one only took him about thirty years to learn!)

Bedrooms are a place for privacy and passion, but also for kindness and consideration. As a couple, you spend more time there, in closer physical contact, than anywhere else. When Cokie reads herself to sleep, she uses a tiny book light that doesn't disturb Steve. Even though Steve prefers the windows open, he keeps them closed because of Cokie's asthma. If Cokie gets to sleep in on Saturdays, Steve puts an extra blanket back on the bed to keep her warm when he leaves for his early-morning tennis game. Then he comes home from tennis with fresh bagels for brunch and makes Cokie her favorite sandwich— topped, in season, with just-sliced, homegrown tomatoes. When Cokie has to leave early for work, she puts her clothes in another room the night before.

> After more than thirty years of marriage, we've learned at least: to listen to each other and understand each other's tastes and habits.

Cokie loves to cook, but once she sits down at the table she's glued to her chair. So if something is forgotten—a wineglass, a serving spoon—it's Steve's job to get it. Normally Steve cleans up after meals, but he also likes to watch his beloved Yankees on TV. Then, Cokie will say, "You're excused; I'll clean up." At other times, she'll put up with a messy kitchen for a while and let Steve do the dishes after the game.

What we're talking about is thoughtfulness, tolerance, generosity—the grease in the gears of family life. A good example might be called the "I'll get it" rule. Whether it's the dog or the doorbell demanding attention, getting up first is usually a good idea. But after a few disruptions, saying "Your turn" is certainly acceptable. Another version is the "What can I get you?" rule. I'm already up, I'm coming home, I'm going out—how can I make your life a bit easier? A corollary is the "You look nice" rule. A word, a touch, a hug, a kiss—anything that expresses appreciation is never a waste. That's particularly true as you get older. When waistlines grow and chins sag, those gestures of affection are more welcome than ever.

Then there's this all-important rule: Make time for each other. We both have a lot of obligations, and it would be easy to go days without sharing a meal or a conversation. Our basic understanding is that we have dinner together whenever possible, and we try to get away occasionally, if only for a day or two, to unplug the wires and focus on each other. Years ago, when we had small kids at home, we escaped for a weekend to San Francisco, and while we were walking along the harbor Cokie looked up and said to Steve, "Have an affair with your wife." It's a maxim we've tried to remember ever since.

Another version of the same idea is the "Stay in touch" rule. We talk many times a day, usually just to say "How did your class go?" or "Try to avoid the construction on Reno Road." Often it's a matter of simple courtesy: "I'm running late" or "Can I pick something up?" When one of us is traveling, we have an agreement: Call when you get in, no matter how late. We've been married more than twelve thousand days, and we've missed talking to each other on no more than a dozen of them.

This business about listening and learning is very important, but sometimes it happens by accident. On our first anniversary, we took a trip to Italy, and after a long, wine-filled lunch we were slogging through the Uffizi Gallery in Florence. We both thought the gallery closed at six, and we were determined to stay until then. But when it closed at five we were thrilled, like kids let out of school early. After that we took longer lunches and shorter tours.

Learning does not have to mean agreeing, or doing everything together. Sometimes it means giving each other the space and support to pursue different interests. Steve likes to go to baseball games with his buddies; Cokie likes to attend church or to lunch with old friends. If Steve is stopping for a beer with his students after class, Cokie might drop by a new mother's hospital room or attend an author's book party.

Sometimes the most generous gesture you can make to your spouse is saying or doing absolutely nothing. We often joke that the success of a marriage can be measured by the number of teeth marks in your tongue. Shared memories add texture and endurance to any long relationship, but forgetting—and forgiving—the bad moments is as important as remembering the good ones.

We have no magic formulas. All couples have to find their own way. But we do know this: Civility makes marriage possible. Call when you're late. Never give your spouse a toaster on your anniversary. And don't forget the flowers.

Dressing for Dinner

by John Mariani

I was having breakfast in the oak-paneled dining room of the historic Hotel Jerome in Aspen when I observed something that quickly put me off my feed. An enchanting little girl, sweetly dressed in a jumper and white leggings, her shining hair carefully pulled back with a barrette, came prancing in. Behind her, trudging into the room like mules, were her parents. The girl's mother was dressed in sweat clothes, and her hair was in need of a good combing. But it was the appearance of the child's father that most brought down this familial tableau. He wore baggy sweats that probably hadn't seen a washday in a while. His sneakers were so worn out that no self-respecting kid would be caught dead in them. But the pièce de résistance was that dreaded symbol of sartorial surrender: the baseball cap worn backward, which he never bothered to remove.

As a restaurant critic for more than a quarter century, I've observed the great dressing-down of America at close range. And I'm sorry to say that men appear to be in the vanguard of this dress-to-regress army.

Not long ago in Paris at the three-star restaurant Arpège, a quartet of free-spending Americans (they ordered a Grand Cru Bordeaux in magnum) arrived wearing nearly identical outfits: pastel-colored tennis shirts, chinos, jogging shoes and those ghastly, ill-named "fanny packs." And recently I watched with a twinge of national shame as a fellow American tried to get into London's

Savoy Grill without a jacket and was cordially, but firmly, forced to wear a gruesome liver-colored number.

While I find such tackiness surprising among people one might expect to take pride in their appearance, I also realize that as the twenty-first century gets under way, American and European society have become much more casual. That is, for the most part, all to the good. The stuffiness that once mandated uncomfortable formal clothes after 6 A.M. is, thankfully, long gone. But for too many men in too many circumstances, casual dress has become slovenly dress. Defenders of such attire in restaurants sometimes point to European men, who dress casually when they go to all but the very finest dining establishments.

There is, however, a difference: When European men—affluent or not—eat out, they still, by and large, dress like *gentlemen*. Even if they've skipped a tie, their look seems more pulled together. That may have something to do with the Continent's exquisite tailoring, extending even to its blue jeans. Still, Europeans seem to be more acutely aware than Americans that certain articles of clothing are simply not worn in certain places. Dressing the part often makes us act the part, and, having had a few more centuries' practice at this, Europeans, generally speaking, tend to more readily recognize the difference between good taste and bad, good tailoring and no tailoring at all.

> For too many men in too many circumstances, casual dress has become slovenly dress.

The fastidious producer-director Sir Alexander Korda once said that any man who would wear a brown hat to town is a cad. How far we have come to a time when a man will not only wear a baseball cap to town but wear it backward in a restaurant. Different times? Yes. Sartorial evolution? Try devolution. (Would that more fellows were as thoughtful in this regard as Joe DiMaggio. The ever-tasteful Yankee Clipper never wore his cap off the field and always entered and left the stadium in an impeccably tailored blue suit, white shirt and a tie.)

Dressing shabbily for any restaurant above the level of a fast-food joint is an affront not only to fellow patrons but to the owner. Unfortunately, many owners themselves have given up, adopting a style of dress that helps make ill-clad customers feel comfortable. At one fashionable restaurant on New York's Upper East Side, the proprietor prides himself on a signature uniform of faded jeans and open-necked shirts. It makes him look more like the fellow who delivers the vegetables than the man who pays for them. While many restaurants still request "appropriate dress" and leave it up to their clientele to figure out what that means, there are a few stalwarts. Sirio Maccioni of New York's Le Cirque 2000 posts a discreet sign at the door that reads: "Jacket and tie are required to enter Le Cirque." Still, some men try to buck the rule, contending that their turtleneck sweater is cashmere or their golf jacket Italian suede, mistaking good fabric for good manners.

Customers who have made the effort to dress appropriately may understandably become offended by the spectacle of carelessly clad patrons. When confronted with barbarians near your plate, there's certainly nothing wrong with politely making your disappointment known to the owner or maître d' upon leaving (or perhaps in a phone call the next day). Dining out, after all, isn't just about the food; it's also about such things as service and ambiance that, taken together, should create a pleasurable experience. Anything that diminishes that experience, especially when you're paying a king's ransom for it, ought to be brought to the restaurant's attention. (And if you're not satisfied with its response, there's nothing that says you have to return.)

For those who suspect that I myself go everywhere buttoned up, I assure you that there are many restaurants I frequent in casual clothes. When I go to a little trattoria in Rome or a bistro in Paris, I probably just throw a sport jacket over my chinos or jeans. And if I'm at a lobster shack in Maine or a barbecue stand in Texas, shorts and a T-shirt seem just about right, maybe with a baseball cap to keep the sun out of my eyes.

Today, many men claim that donning a jacket and tie is a form of strangulation, even though they've survived years in their white-collar jobs without any apparent loss of breath. To them I say, buy a larger-size shirt and learn to tie your tie. (I happen to find jackets wonderfully convenient for storing everything from eyeglasses to pens, and there's always the chance a woman might feel a chill and need my suit coat or blazer around her shoulders.) Others say they should be permitted to wear anything they please to a restaurant, maintaining that their money is as good as that of any guy in a coat and tie. Such logic suggests an arrogance about privilege that's no more attractive today than it's ever been. It also reflects a total misunderstanding of how the impression you make affects your surroundings: You can either stand out in a crowded dining room because you're well dressed or stand out like a sore thumb.

Clothes may not make the man, but slovenly dress definitely unmakes him. On the other hand, dress that is appropriate to the restaurant in question shows a person respects his hosts, guests and fellow diners. And, perhaps most important of all, it serves as a model to our children—rather than the other way around.

Respecting Our Elders

·— by Anne Taylor Fleming ·—

I t seemed a small thing. As my mother and I crossed a street we had crossed a thousand times before—jaywalking, I have to admit—I reached out and gently took her elbow in some sort of instinctively protective gesture. It happened fast. There was no forethought. My mother is an elegant, smart, fully capable woman who has slowed down slightly in the past few years, but only slightly. Still, something in that day, some apprehension, some something, caused me to reach for her, as forty-odd years before she would have reached for my hand as we crossed the very same street.

The symbolic poetry of it all was not, it turns out, on my mother's mind. Dignity was. She shook me off firmly and reached the other side of the street resolutely solo. We said nothing about it, but I got the message. Don't patronize me, she was saying, as loudly as if she'd shouted it. And I realized that my good intentions were indeed laced with the first hint of that role-reversing patronization: child as mother, mother as child. Where did it come from? I, who pride myself on trying, at least, to be sensitive, had failed the test, had fallen into the trap of regarding someone older as someone less than—someone in need of my still-sturdy midlife hand.

Ever since I have been conscious of not committing the same mistake, conscious of the slights and biases of the world around me toward the older among us. I'm not referring to hard-core abuse—the stuff of grisly news stories; I'm talking about more subtle matters—the finger-drumming impatience when an aging parent doesn't get in or out of a car or get to a punch line as quickly as in the days of yore. Little things. Little hurtful things. Again, this is not full-tilt cruelty, but it's cruel nonetheless, part of the humming refrain of insult and insensitivity that buzzes just under our youth-obsessed culture.

No question, the U.S. is a tough place in which to grow old. We have no tradition of respecting our elders as other cultures do. In fact, quite the contrary. We embrace the new, the hot, the hip, the happening. We don't look back; we look forward. Some of that, of course, is our strength, built right into the marrow of the country, which only became one by throwing off the parental paw of England. But the healthy aspects of that American-bred attitude, I think, have gone too far and become unhealthy, a dismissive view of anyone and everyone over a certain age. We don't avail ourselves of their wisdom, their humor.

When I was a very new bride, in my early twenties, I fell in with two gentlemen in their sixties. They were among the first tight circle of friends my husband and I made as newlyweds. They taught me to drink old-fashioneds and smoke cigars—remember, this was eons before that

> We have no tradition of respecting our elders as other cultures do. In fact, quite the contrary. We embrace the new, the hot, the hip, the happening.

became trendy—and laugh at life in a way foreign to my young soul. I was in such a hurry to be something and somebody. They had long since done it all—romance, kids, career—and understood full well that a good cigar, a big belly laugh and a jitterbug were worth a fortune. They gave me a gift far beyond their love and friendship: a whole other perspective. That's something nobody younger could possibly have given me.

And that's what we lose when we relegate our elders to some distant corner of our lives: a different perspective. So many, too many, of the people I know do that. Caught between young children they had late and the hungry demands of careers, they don't have time for grandparents or other older relatives and friends, except for those special photo-op events like graduations or weddings or the occasional golf game (grudgingly played). So we start to see our elders as a breed apart, people to be tolerated or helped across the street rather than people to enjoy and hang out with and listen to and shop with and treat like equals.

It is, for all concerned, a lonesome way to live.

Say "Thank You"

by Catherine Calvert

You'll probably think I'm ruthless. After all, he was only a teenager and he'd rarely spent any time with me. But I was cross. For the fifteenth year in a row, I'd chosen and wrapped and mailed that godson a birthday present, and chosen and wrapped and mailed him a Christmas present and watched my mailbox for months, never clapping eyes on a thank-you note. He was excused for lack of literacy in those first few years, but after that I'd have settled for a badly spelled sentence and a crayoned drawing. And by the time he was in boarding school, he surely could have scraped together a word or two. Call me prissy, but that was it. He was off the gift list forever.

These days, thanks of any sort can be as rare as an empty taxi in the rain. Is that because our lives are full? Certainly, we're all terribly, terribly busy, bolting from job to party to bed, feeling like so many hamsters hauling ourselves around a wheel. Ignorance? Some of us were otherwise engaged (picketing? getting MBAs?) when the chapter on how to write a thank-you letter was discussed. Sheer obliviousness? "Spoiled children," maintains one friend of mine, who's a mistress of certitude. "The more you have, the less you appreciate it."

I'm not suggesting a return to a Little House on the Prairie world, where a penny and an orange in a child's Christmas stocking was the nineteenth-century equivalent of a trip to FAO Schwarz.

But it is tempting to wonder whether those of any age to whom much is given begin to accept all things bright and beautiful as a matter of course. ("It's always interesting to see whose children come up with the thank-you letters after a party," says another friend, whose little girl is a regular on the New York City party circuit, where a tidal wave of toys greets the happy birthday child. "It's not always the ones who were born with monogrammed paper who use it.") Or could it be that our modern flood of messages—beeping answering machines, words from our sponsor, notes from the PTA, 122 channels and a mailbox that needs an annex—tends to devalue any impulse to communicate?

I'm not about to set myself up as a pinkie-raised arbiter of behavior, but surely something's lost when a gesture of thanks is omitted. Making the most of such a gesture can be one of life's purest pleasures, in which the truly imaginative transmute the "chore" into something special—the most basic form of communication, heart to heart.

Of course, I'd been an offender as a thankless youth. I remember bogging down while working my way through a very long list of wedding-present thank-yous. The first few were buoyed by the joy of using stationery with my new initials, the next hundred a connect-the-dots exercise in getting the job done. But almost at the end, I petered out. It took a call from Tiffany & Co., gently inquiring whether I'd actually received the five china plates because the donor was concerned, to send me back to my desk. There I concocted an abject apology and fulsome thanks, after rejecting all sorts of alternatives, like moving overseas. I winced for months whenever I encountered that woman of a certain age, gracious to her gloved fingertips, who'd seen my seamy, sloppy side.

As the years went by and I became a wife, a worker and a hostess, I found gratitude had all sorts of themes and variations. And I learned to take greater pleasure in extending thanks as my joy in receiving thanks grew. I reveled, for example, after a dinner party, when—within just a few days—my mailbox would be full of thank-yous. Some would be written on paper so stiff it crunched; others came in the form of a postcard from the Met or the Louvre, the handwriting attesting to its having been scribbled on a knee in a cab.

A friend wins the promptness award: My husband and I were only just drying the glassware when I heard a noise at the front door. Under it, a white envelope appeared, inch by inch, followed by the sound of receding footsteps. It was a thank-you note written just forty-five minutes after the sender's departure. Besides a really good postparty hash session about the guests and the food and the funny thing somebody said, such notes are part of the ritual, if you will, of the dinner. And I save them along with the menu, souvenirs of an evening that went well.

> The thank-you ought to match the present. The person who surprises you with a birthday party deserves the note, yes, but also a gesture that more accurately corresponds with his generosity.

Of course, I have taken pleasure in other sorts of thanks. There was the well-chosen book from a friend we'd put up for a club membership. Not to mention the weekend guest who showed his gratitude by arriving with the makings of a lobster dinner, down to the clawed guest of honor. (He also gave us the gift of time: He cooked.) There were the fancy lunches from acquaintances who were grateful for job referrals. And how well I recall a thank-you note from an antiques dealer that came attached to the most heartbreakingly romantic bundle of pink rosebuds in a fine porcelain cup. It was so personal and yet so appropriate.

With the memory of such gestures ever fresh, I never mind the trek to find the perfect thank-you for a kindness someone has shown me. I have a file with the number of the florist whose bouquets look fresh-gathered from a meadow, and the candymaker who still knows how to make butterscotch. (For some reason I've decided that is the answer to almost any difficult search.) I always like imagining the recipients' faces when they untie the flowers or open the box. Indeed, it is in becoming more sensitive to the gift giver—the person who sets this would-be exchange in motion— that you learn an important lesson about proportion: the thank-you ought to match the present. The person who surprises you with a birthday party deserves the note, yes, but also a gesture that more accurately corresponds with his generosity.

"Only connect," E.M. Forster said, and that's the essence of grateful gestures. The best ones offer up a tangible sign that someone took note—discovered the books laid carefully beside a weekender's bed, appreciated the spring flowers searched out in the dead of winter. One friend listened hard when a woman told of her love for birch trees, and then to repay an act of immense kindness, went out and bought her an entire grove of them.

No, we can't all give trees, yet how often a single sheet of paper would do. Since so little can go such a long way, it's a pity more of us can't find the wherewithal for some form of requital. Because in the end, any response is better than none at all, even if expressed in glowing green letters on a computer screen, or a quick phone call or a lilting message on an answering machine. Sometimes it's merely a matter of practicality: I want to know whether a package arrived, if a friend really liked the play or if everyone survived my interesting foray into Chilean cuisine so artfully served in that pumpkin.

How I love receiving a letter or card I can read in my own time and reread when I feel like it, or a gift that brings certain pleasures to mind: the plant that will survive memory of the details or the music box with a song that brings back every detail. Maybe it's the pound of good coffee that memorializes all the cups we've drunk together, or the photo from a vacation, enlarged and framed, that glows long after the sunburn fades.

Without a thank-you, the cycle of gift giving is incomplete. Something pleasurable, but also something fundamental, is lost when expediency is chosen over form. If poetry is emotion recollected in tranquillity, then surely a gesture of thanks can be a perfect poem.

III
FAMILY AFFAIRS

*Funny how our nearest and dearest
can test us the most—and give us our best opportunities
to show what we're made of.*

Keeping It in the Family

by Sue Miller

There were several years during my son's adolescence when virtually any question I asked him was treated with the scalding contempt that is the specialty of the teenager. "Why are you so interested?" "I really don't want to talk about that with you." Or, worst of all, because it was designed to make me aware of how very tedious a person I was to deal with: "Why do you always have to ask that?" (This in response to something like "Did you have a good time?")

Of course, I was glad when this stage passed, but at certain times in later life I've wondered about it—the adolescent impulse to keep everything, every tiny little thing, secret. Not so much where it comes from, because I think we all remember the sense we had at that age that any shared information was a kind of capitulation to the whole adult agenda, but where it goes to in our brave new world.

Perhaps in days of yore it was a stage in the development of that old-fashioned virtue, discretion. Perhaps it led directly to the kinds of silence that adult society demanded about a whole range of things. One didn't speak of sexuality in public then, as one didn't speak of pregnancy, or cancer, or those who drank too much or who coveted their neighbors' wives. Or their oxen or asses, for that matter. Now it seems we can't get enough of exactly this kind of information about each other. Look at the smashing success of the memoir of one's own pathology—clear testimony to this. But it makes you ask yourself what happened to that instinct, if it was an instinct, to keep your mouth shut. Whatever happened to family secrets?

It's not that I would wish back that WASPy world where nothing of any personal importance could be discussed either within or outside the family. I grew up in such a world, and I know too well its sometimes paralyzing impact. But there were virtues there that got discarded along with the clearer limitations, and one of them was, I think, the sense of a right to personal privacy, especially within the family.

It's easy to blame Freud. In the name of freeing ourselves from that contemporary bogeyman he invented, repression, we've taken to a kind of determined honesty about everything, varyingly called confessing or clearing the air or sharing or letting it all hang out. We've seen the most debased versions of this in public forums: Jenny Jones, Jerry Springer, et al. But there are more familiar versions, too, ones that perhaps we've stopped noticing but might do well to think about again.

At dinner parties, even among casual acquaintances, we've all, I suspect, fielded the most egregiously intimate questions, posed with every expectation that we should have no objection to answering fully. And if you don't? If you resist? Then, my dear, you are the one perceived as rude. And not just rude, but that even more damning adjective, uptight. For if openness is a kind of summum bonum in our culture, then reserve becomes repression and the wish for privacy a symptom of neurosis.

In my own enormous extended family I have a relative, who shall remain nameless, who has resisted this sense of repression by insisting on a kind of brutal truth telling, making confidences public, pointing out every evasion or the implications of passive-aggressive remarks. ("Don't you see what you're really saying here?") To clear the air, that's always the stated goal. Because, after all, where are we supposed to reveal ourselves? Where are we completely honest? Where does it all hang out? The family, right? Where you know, even as also you are known. I remember reading Susan Cheever's indignation at her father's concealing from her his bisexuality, her feeling that this secret compromised him as a man, as a writer, but most of all as a father.

Well, of course, she had every right to feel that way. But I can think of many reasons for a man to wish to keep such a thing from a child, among them the most loving, the most protective, the most paternal. Perhaps Cheever's reasons were not any of these things. I can't know that. But I think even within the family there is no need for the honesty that could wound uselessly, the confession that benefits the confessor—by making him feel less guilty, or perhaps even virtuous, for his great honesty—at the expense of the person the confession torments. In my family, the outing of secrets others weren't ready to confront never worked as it was intended to, never led to that new, more open and healthy life.

Let's use the real Freud here against his popularized version. If we look more closely at what he says, we see that he didn't ever argue against suppression. In fact, in a general sense, he found it absolutely necessary. For in his dynamic view of life, it's out of sublimated emotion that we work, that we achieve, that we build civilization at all. And what is the family, if not a miniature civilization? The very place, in fact, in which we're supposed to learn civility.

And within which, whether we're conscious of it or not, we

practice discretion all the time. We edit our murderous thoughts about our children. We don't mention the hatred we temporarily feel for a spouse when we know that it will pass, that it's born of some difficulty of the moment. We live in our bodies and don't speak much of what goes on with them, even to our most beloved. The family secret can be an extension of this kind of discretion: the loving silence about things which it does not help the others to know, the private treasuring of the personal details of intimacy, the looking away from what is painful and can't be changed to what distracts or uplifts or amuses.

I'll tell a tale on my grandparents here, since they're both long gone. Shortly after my first novel, *The Good Mother*, came out, my grandfather, surely the most competitive man who ever walked the earth, felt the need to apprise me that he knew fully as much about sex as I did (for that was his offended understanding of what my book was exclusively about). Offended or not, he wanted his victory, and so he began, over a picnic lunch, to speak

> We live in our bodies and don't speak much of what goes on with them, even to our most beloved.

loudly of the intimate details of his life with my grandmother, who blanched and blushed, and then, as if to call him back to a better self, put her hand on his arm and said, "None of us has the least idea what you're speaking of, David." And changed the subject.

It was nicely done, and a reminder that it can be done, gracefully and lovingly. As John Cheever's character Honora Wapshot said when things got sticky in her world, "Feel that lovely breeze!" And sometimes a secret, a silence, is just that: a lovely breeze. A different and often more effective way of clearing the air.

Nagging Habits

by Susan Dundon

y husband and I and another couple have gathered at our house and are about to leave for a wedding. It strikes me, suddenly, as my husband helps me into my coat, that what he's wearing is absolutely, unequivocally wrong. Everything that I know about How to Behave in the World According to My Mother tells me not to be a nag about this. I will certainly not risk ruining an entire evening over my husband's choice of attire.

No sooner is this resolve firmly planted in my mind than my mouth springs open, as if someone has yanked a string at the back of my neck. "Why," I ask, "are you wearing a blazer, as if you're going to a brunch? It's an evening wedding." I make my point at least twice more in rapid succession, leaving my poor husband no time to offer an explanation.

Rather than change into a suit, he sweeps me out of the house so swiftly that my feet do not touch the ground. Our friends, mute in the middle of a potentially explosive situation, shuffle silently out the door. By now, the atmosphere is completely contaminated. None of us is in the mood for a wedding.

I take no pride in relating this incident, casting me as it does in such an unflattering light. But I'm reminded of it whenever I'm aware of someone nagging his spouse, partner, child, sibling or friend. It may be just my imagination, but if I seem to be noticing it more, perhaps it's because, in this day of full and public disclosure, zipping one's lip seems like a lost art. All that assertiveness training of the past decade or so didn't help us become more genteel.

To be sure, there can be a fine line between nagging and what could be construed as constructive criticism. Though we may not be able to pin down the perfect definition of nagging, we recognize it when we hear it. Tone of voice is one distinguishing feature. One's grievance is often registered at a higher-than-normal frequency, not unlike that of a smoke alarm. Then there's the persistence. Once is never enough, is it, when asking a teenager to please not sprawl across the dinner table. (Variations might include withering stares or barely audible badgering.) And nagging can sometimes be defined by the number of people who—along with its intended target— have to endure it. As part of that captive audience, we want only to escape, to head off into the woods like Rip Van Winkle for a twenty-year reprieve.

Nagging may be bad enough behind a family's closed doors, but in public, there's no doubt about it: Nagging is pollution, and everyone within breathing distance is either hurt or made to feel ill at ease. Our children hold it against us. Our friends avoid us. Our spouses think of George or Martha in *Who's Afraid of Virginia Woolf?* and wish us dead.

Not long ago, I spent an evening in the company of a man whose wife had caused us to be late for a movie. Being late is, in fact, his wife's signature trait, otherwise lovable though she is. She was profuse in her apologies, but her husband would not let it go.

She was rude, he insisted. She was inconsiderate. She did it on purpose. The movie itself was but a brief interlude, like passing under a bridge during a downpour. The credits rolled silently, and then the storm continued. It made my toes curl in my shoes.

If we know what nagging is, we also know what it is not. It is not helpful. As a confirmed member of the Wardrobe Police, I can almost always sense even as I phrase the question "Is that what you're going to wear?" that my entreaty probably won't bring about the desired result.

But if nagging is generally so ineffective, why do you suppose we even bother? My theory is that most of us honestly believe we have the other person's best interests at heart. We nag loved ones, for example, about their eating habits. Why? To prevent their dying prematurely of more than the recommended daily requirement of French fries. Or we endlessly pester our teenagers about choosing a career, because we want them to enjoy their work, to have a sense of fulfillment, to be happy. We do it for them. We could save ourselves so much embarrassment if only we would anticipate the problem and hash it out beforehand—in the bedroom, in the car, on the walk to church—or bite our tongues until later and talk about it when we're once again alone. Or, when a nagging jag is coming on, we might simply excuse ourselves. Powder rooms, especially those with fans, are excellent at-home spaces for this purpose. The downside to this solution is that it takes a great deal of self-control, which probably accounts for why so few people manage to do it.

If you're in the nagger's hapless audience, walking away can be effective, even dramatic, if done with aplomb. But when that isn't possible, we might try diverting everyone's attention to something else, anything else, or injecting a little comic relief. I recall an occasion when a congenial group of old friends were out to dinner. We were having a jolly time until the dessert cart came by. One of the men, who is, by his own admission, at least twenty pounds overweight, selected so many offerings that it might have been more practical to leave the cart with our friend and carry the remaining desserts away on a small plate.

His wife, ever mindful of her husband's excesses, was incredulous. Her eyes cut a path to each mouthful like the black dotted line in the "Nancy" comics. He seemed determined to ignore her. She nudged his arm. She squirmed in her seat. She muttered under her breath. All to no avail. A hush fell over the table as, heads bowed, we all concentrated fiercely on our own assorted gastronomic indiscretions.

Now why couldn't one of us have done the gracious thing and helped out by bringing up something compelling from that day's headlines or by telling a joke? Even if none of us had found it funny, we certainly would have laughed. We needed to laugh.

Maybe next time.

Meanwhile, my husband and I have received another invitation to a wedding. I can hardly wait to see what he's going to wear. Whatever it is, not a word will pass my lips. That's a promise.

A Single Parent's Say

— · by Véronique Vienne · —

hilip and I make a great team when we travel," said the woman in the lilac cardigan to whom I'd just been introduced at a cocktail party. "He takes care of the passports and the tickets, while I keep my eyes on the map."

"I know what you mean," I responded, eager to join the conversation. "A man will do anything to avoid asking for directions."

"Oh, Philip is my ten-year-old son," she said, adding softly: "I'm a single mother."

It might have occurred to me not to assume that Philip was the woman's husband: I'm a single mother, too. Divorced when my daughter was four, I was the sole custodian of her childhood. And even though she's now an adult and I am remarried, I'm obviously not above the occasional relapse, conditioned, like most people, I suppose, to view traditional mom-and-dad imagery as the sterling parental template. Alas, my own state of parenthood without marital partner did not automatically come with lifetime membership to a sensitivity club.

When I think about how easy it is, even for a veteran, to stumble, I begin to appreciate what people who haven't been exposed to the realities of single parenting must sometimes go through in social situations. I think of a friend, for example, who was introduced to a colleague's daughter and nonchalantly said to his coworker, "I didn't know you were married." (She wasn't.) Or people who meet my new husband and ask him all about my daughter, as if he were her father.

These missteps hardly constitute high crimes and misdemeanors. But even the most well-intentioned among us can be slow to catch up with modern realities. As Nancy E. Dowd, professor at the University of Florida College of Law and the author of *In Defense of Single-Parent Families*, explained: "Expressions like 'unwed mothers' or 'broken families' still haunt us." And yet, a few estimates suggest that up to 70 percent of children will spend some time in a single-parent family before reaching the age of eighteen.

Today, the term "single parent" might describe a galaxy of scenarios, including divorced or widowed moms and dads, unmarried people who adopt and even single women who choose artificial insemination. Still, as Professor Dowd acknowledges, that seemingly innocent term "single" is far from neutral. "It appears to remove the condemnation," she writes, "yet its meaning and connotations [can lead to] the persistence of stigma."

That stigma may reflect society's strong belief in the institution of marriage: If marriage is the ideal, then there must be something less than ideal about raising children outside of it. Subtly, subconsciously, that attitude polarizes us. We simply cannot imagine that children can be happy having two homes instead of one. So, single parents can be reluctant to extol the pleasures of raising children solo. It might come across as self-indulgent or even unseemly. This could explain why married parents sometimes pity their single counterparts. If only they knew just how often children of single parents establish great, lasting partnerships with their fathers or mothers.

Like the precocious son of the woman I met at the cocktail party, my daughter was a responsible and capable youngster. Not only did she keep track of the expiration dates on passports and milk cartons, but she also, as an adolescent, monitored the mileage on the car between oil changes. "I don't know where you'd be now if it hadn't been for me," she remarked once, at the end of her teens. Next thing I knew she was off to Vassar, confident that she had done a good job of raising us both.

Indeed, research shows that a strong sense of responsibility and self-confidence is not uncommon among boys and girls who grow up in one-adult households. There have been times when I'd love to have shouted out that fact, probably after someone at lunch, or maybe the hairdresser, asked about my daughter in downright sympathetic tones. In my more devious moments, I've wanted to reply, "She has a single mother, not a disease."

> We simply cannot imagine that children can be happy having two homes instead of one. So, single parents can be reluctant to extol the pleasures of raising children solo.

As vexing as some comments about marital status may be, they are less unnerving than the studious silence that sometimes surrounds the topic of single parenting. A friend who takes her children to Nantucket every August experienced a definite cooling in the air after her divorce. Women with whom she'd spent many afternoons at the beach club acted strangely absentminded in her presence. "They were my childhood playmates; we formed a close-knit matriarchal community of summer moms," she recalls. "All of a sudden, they were unable to have a normal conversation with me. They didn't even inquire about my kids' new school."

To be sure, most single parents are never subjected to the form of censure my friend encountered. Far less stinging, though no less annoying, is the misconception that single parents are eager for their friends to play matchmaker. "Married people often assume that you would rather go out on a blind date than stay home with your children," says a fetching ex-wife I know. "Their mistake, I guess, is to believe that children raised by one parent are screaming brats. I hate to disappoint them, but my son and daughter make charming dinner companions."

Single parenting, of course, is not exactly a new phenomenon. But because its world, historically speaking, still has plenty of uncharted territory, thoughtful visitors should proceed with care. Their next social blunder could be just around the corner, unless they take that important moment to refrain from making easy assumptions. For example, that nice father you met at the club might be delighted to drop by for drinks, even if all your other guests are couples. The so-called "odd man out" (talk about negative expressions) may simply appreciate being asked out. And, please, wait until you know the fellow better before introducing him to your recently divorced friends.

There are times in all battles for greater social sensitivity, though, when the best course is retreat. I was reminded of this one day when my ex-mother-in-law came to dinner. (We've become good friends; my divorce from her son took place more than a quarter-century ago.) After the meal, we shared a reflective moment. "Your daughter turned out to be such a fine young woman," she said with a pleasant sigh. "I don't know how she managed."

Oh well, I thought, let it go. She did get the most important point: Her granddaughter is a fine young woman.

Missing the Point

by Patricia Beard

Five of us were having lunch at the beach club one sunny summer day. Four of us knew each other well. Although we knew the fifth in a way—had watched her at golf lessons and swimming in the ocean—we'd never really talked with her. That day was no exception. The woman who'd brought her along proceeded to ignore her, and for more than an hour the conversation was conducted as though this extra guest weren't there. Toward the end of lunch, she finally interrupted and said, in a voice mined with hostility, "Can I go now?" We looked at her, perhaps for the first time, and words like "sullen" and "bratty" floated through my mind. But I reconsidered.

As you may have guessed, the object of our lapse in civility that day was a child, a ten-year-old whose play date had been canceled at the last minute. While I can't say I cared for her rudeness, I have to sympathize with a child who was plunged into an adult environment and treated like an unwanted pickle on a plate.

How would I feel, I asked myself, if I were the recipient of this kind of oblivious rudeness? What if I were to go to a party where I didn't know the other guests and the couple who brought me abandoned me to make my own way for the evening? Or what if, while I was in a store, my shopping companion stopped to talk to a friend, failed to introduce me, then chatted for ten minutes while I stood around like a log? How about having dinner with friends at a restaurant where the meal dragged on until I was too tired to eat?

"I'm ready to leave," I might say. Wouldn't I feel resentful if the others snapped "Well, we're not"?

When young people interrupt and disrupt, grown-ups are apt to mutter, "What's the matter with kids today?" Perhaps a better question is, What's wrong with the adults who set their children up to be uncomfortable, then embarrass them further when they act badly? People who wouldn't dream of imposing such inconsiderate behavior on their peers are somehow not averse to giving their children short shrift in the manners department.

Most of us have witnessed examples of this double standard. A man who would never insist that his wife sit on the sidelines and watch him play two sets of tennis parks his eight-year-old son on the grass by the side of the court. Surprise: Halfway through the match, the boy begins to whine. But who's really spoiled? The father might have been able to find another child to keep his son company while he played, or he might have mitigated the boy's impatience by giving him something to look forward to—promising that when the game was over, they'd have their own fifteen minutes hitting balls. (The court's booked? Well, then they can practice together against the backboard.)

What's wrong with the adults who set their children up to be uncomfortable, then embarrass them further when they act badly?

A woman who would never be an hour late to meet her husband stops to do some errands and picks up her daughter from a party long after the other young guests have gone home. The little girl, worried that she's been forgotten, greets her mother with a fresh remark. The mother's reaction is to scold her—in front of the hostess. (Of course she and her husband never argue in public: "That's different.") A parent who is unavoidably detained should, at least, call the hostess, then talk to the child, telling her when she expects to arrive. (And when the child becomes a teenager, her parents will be glad they set a good example when she calls to say that she'll be half an hour late.)

I know quite a few little folks, as young as two or three, who mind their manners in a heart-gladdening way—less formally, perhaps, than children once did, but with respect. I've noticed that their parents treat them the same way. By contrast, the children I've seen snarling with bad humor are often just mimicking the rudeness that's been directed toward them—often by their parents.

What has turned otherwise polite adults into parents who are so careless with their children in social settings? Certain developments come to mind. One is the ubiquity of work; if the time you can spend with a child is mostly concentrated on the weekends, when you also want to see friends, you try to combine the two, sometimes with unfortunate results. A related issue is the scarcity of good child minders. When parents can't find a reliable babysitter, adults and children are thrown together in circumstances that don't quite fit either age group.

There is, too, the matter of power. The obsession with success slips into our social interactions, which brings to mind the horrible word networking. We've all seen men and women at parties who are polite to those who can help them in some way and cool to those who can't. If we think of everyone we see as contributing to our success or our status, the pressure to be "on" all the time is overwhelming. Then when we have to let down our guard and blow off some steam, too often the only safe place to do so is around our kids, over whom we hold the power.

The solution to this dilemma is not for parents to run their lives around their children, or to make children the center of attention in mixed-age situations; a person can't play Pin the Tail on the Donkey all night just because eight-year-olds are included in the party. A sensible parent might have thought to bring along either toys or books that would engage a child during the gathering. Surely, one can't expect children to be gracious and understanding when their parents treat them in a way that lacks grace or understanding—the linchpins of good manners.

You and I, of course, do not do such things to our offspring. But when others of our acquaintance treat their children like dogs left outside without a bowl of water on a hot day, there's nothing to stop us from showing a little kindness. If you notice young Annabel wandering around at a party, evidently finding it hard to connect with others her age, you can spend a few minutes trying to help her get settled, perhaps by asking the other children about the game they're playing, then suggesting a part for her. When you meet a friend with her son in a store, you can cut the conversation short if you notice that the child is restless, perhaps by saying that you don't want to interfere with the family outing.

I agree with the maxim that it takes a village to raise a child; and that includes showing, by word and deed, what courtesy looks like. We are sure to see the benefits in children who are sunnier, more open—and more polite. And we might not have to listen to the plaints of a child whose parents are saving their good manners for those who could walk away from them if *they* were rude.

Grand (Parent) Expectations

by Anne Bernays

I tried hard to be cool about the looming first grandchild—the first of five boys—but my unconscious tricked me into misreading the nameplate on a Pontiac as "Grand Ma" when it was clearly "Grand Am." This psychic dyslexia was a reminder that the desire for grandchildren can be nearly as urgent as the desire for children. It took my husband somewhat longer to get used to the idea. At first, whenever someone mentioned the grandfather thing, he looked distraught, like Shirley MacLaine in *Terms of Endearment* when she finds out her daughter's pregnant ("Not me!"). Most of us eventually experience this yearning that settles in the chest like heartburn. It hits soon after our children marry. Maybe we need to know that trickles of our DNA, as well as our dazzling personalities and talents, will turn up in a new generation—an acceptable exercise of amour propre. But genetic pride can't be the whole story, or why would adopted grandchildren bring on the same throat-closing affection? Hearing "Oh hi, Grandma, when are you coming to see us?" on the phone can make my day.

In bygone times, old folks were seen as both cheeky and wise. Kids listened to their grandparents; sat on their laps; learned card tricks and fly tying from grandpa, pie baking and the art of flirtation from grandma; and discovered that making a little mischief wasn't automatically going to lead to a death sentence. Grandparents sprang happy surprises, helped negotiate family differences, demonstrated graceful table manners. They were as much a fixture in a family's life as the dog was. But that situation no longer holds true, at least not in my family.

Today, a lot of grandparents—especially those like us, whose nearest of three daughters lives thirty-five miles away and whose farthest, one thousand—are often at a loss about what to do with our considerable grandparent energy. We would like to be the sharp old owls of the family but are too often only a voice on the telephone. Add to the distance problem the fact that children are not merely scheduled for daily after-school activities but are also programmed up to the ears—soccer, baseball, art school, gymnastics, clarinet lessons, you name it—and it's easy to see why grandparents register so faintly on a child's horizon. We're reduced to counting on holidays, a Sunday or two, birthdays, a wedding or a funeral. How do you maintain constancy without becoming a major pest?

At times, it seems, the only thing to do is to apply directly for an invitation. "Well," says Susanna, "if you want to come and watch David play baseball . . . better bring a folding chair." (Susanna is proud of her children's accomplishments, on and off the diamond. She phones to read me their celestial report cards. She also understands that my principal value as a grandmother is as an emotional booster—"Tell Grandma about your trip to Ellis Island"—rather than as anything more practical.)

It's even hard to entice the boys to our house, but when we do they like being here. We have a cupboard of toys and games. We stroll around the town. We visit a local museum crammed with dinosaur bones, stuffed animals and a superior gift shop. We buy ice cream in Harvard Square. I can't remember more than a couple of times when I've told them "No" or even "Later." They don't test us, because there's no need to. But if they lived with us, we'd have to attach them to the parental leash.

My mother, who often dispensed questionable advice, claimed it was possible to buy love. Of course you can't buy love, but you can make a grandchild sit up and smile by giving him something. It doesn't take much: a bag of Gummi Bears, a seashell, a key ring that lights up. The size, shape or value of the gift is irrelevant, so long as he comprehends the powerful feelings behind the gesture.

To be a truly stellar grandparent, I suppose what you do is remember what it was about your own that you loved most, then try to emulate it. My favorite was Oma Hattie, my mother's mother. She taught me how to play gin rummy and canasta. I used to visit her almost every Saturday at the Mayflower Hotel in New York, where she made me egg-salad sandwiches; after lunch we would play cards for hours. I can't remember her ever telling me what to do or scolding me or suggesting that I wasn't anything but the best company she had enjoyed all week—and she had scores of friends. What Oma Hattie taught me (along with card sense) was that when the time came, I should try my best not to be a parent to my grandchildren.

> Grandparents can only view the ad hoc nature of their grandchildren's lives as evidence of profound social change.

If forced to pick one principle of good grandparenting, I would say don't meddle. The worst case of grandmother meddling I've ever heard of involved a woman who, while minding her five-year-old granddaughter for the day, cut off the child's long hair without asking the mother if it was OK. (It wasn't.)

My father's mother, Oma Anna, sticks to the flypaper of my

memory not because she was particularly nice but because she was so trenchant. (She once told me, "Siggy was such a clever man," referring to her brother, Dr. Freud, of whom she was both proud and envious.) But even Anna refrained from inserting herself between my sister and me and our parents.

When I was growing up, our family thrived on regularity: set times, places and conduct for meals, afternoon naps, bedtimes, social obligations. As young parents, my husband and I bagged most of the rules we both were raised on. We ate in the kitchen, let the girls choose their own clothes (one of them never wore a dress until the day she graduated from high school), allowed them what, to our parents, would have been unthinkable liberties. And now? Grandparents can only view the ad hoc nature of their grandchildren's lives as evidence of profound social change. Teens no longer seem to date; they get their thrills, en masse, cruising the mall. Parents bring their kids along to dinner parties and restaurants. "Manners" have become "attitude," and, paradoxically, although people are living far longer than they did a century ago, grandparents have to fight for airtime with their grandchildren.

But should I fret if my grandsons don't stand up when I come into the room? No. It's far more important to make a psychic connection with these five adorable boys than it is to have them bow when they see me. Making that connection takes some creative noodling. For instance, I've been compiling a list of items commonplace fifty or sixty years ago, things my grandchildren wouldn't recognize. (Now up to eighty-two, it includes such objects as giant ice tongs, carbon paper, snoods and darning eggs.) I'm waiting patiently for the boys to ask me to deconstruct the list for them. I think it will take at least a couple of overnights—at our place.

With All Due Respect

— • by Stacey Okun • —

We were waddling down the street, minding our own business—my baby, who was completing his eighth month in utero, and me—when a woman interrupted my reverie with a tap on the shoulder. "It's a girl," she said, smiling a bit too intimately.

"No," I said calmly, without breaking my stride, "it's a boy."

"Na-ah," she said in a singsong voice, "I can tell from the way you're carrying, it's a girl, honey. You're having a girl."

"Listen to me," I said through gritted teeth, "I had an amnio. I had a sonogram. I saw a certain defining body part. It's a boy. I know for sure."

"Well," she said in a huff, "why'd you have to go and find out?" And with that, she crossed the street.

I'm still not sure why I bothered to respond to the woman. My husband chalks it up to hormones going astray, but I knew deep inside that this complete stranger had unwittingly tapped into a secret fear: that the test results were somehow mistaken and, although I'd gotten excited about the idea of having a boy, I'd actually be having a girl. The night after this incident, I had a dream in which my mother and I (moments after delivering my unexpected daughter) tore out of the hospital and hailed a cab to Bloomingdale's, to start exchanging the blue booties for the pink ones.

At this writing, I'm two weeks away from my due date, the first such date of my life that doesn't mean an article is due on an editor's desk. Yet even though I'm no expert on pregnancy, there's one thing I can say with absolute certainty: The minute a woman starts showing, her belly becomes everybody's belly; her fetus and his gender, health, future hair color and higher-education options are prime topics for everyone's opinion. In fact, as my friend Marnie reports, "pregnancy intrusion" begins even before conception: "People started asking me at my wedding when I was going to have a baby."

There is no code of ethics to follow when responding to people's invasive if often well-meaning comments about your fertility, your growing girth once you've conceived or the way you behave during pregnancy. Snappy comebacks are helpful, but pregnancy tends to sap many of your witty brain cells, replacing them with others that dreamily ponder the lullabies you'll croon to your newborn. This, I was told by a cashier at the local bagel shop, is called "pregnancy brain," as in, "You just gave me a twenty-dollar bill for two sesame bagels and didn't wait for your change."

I'm willing to admit that I've suffered from pregnancy brain, devilish hormone swings and just about every other prenatal phenomenon known to woman (such as a craving for large chocolate-chip cookies, with the chips baked in—not on top). These stresses haven't always put me in the right frame of mind for handling nosy, inappropriate or just plain bizarre behavior. But there are ways to deal with the following questions, comments and situations, that will become as much a part of pregnancy as Pampers will to postpartum life (the start of another round of unsolicited commentary).

How long did it take you to get pregnant? Of course, the answer to this query is your business alone—but don't say that. Instead, look him (or, more likely, her) in the eye, smile and say, "The perfect amount of time, thank you very much."

Do you know the baby's sex? If you're not keeping it a secret, by all means, share your news. But be prepared to hear, "Oh, a boy! Your husband must be so excited." (And I'm not? And he wouldn't be if it were a girl?) Or, as somebody remarked to my friend Lauren, "You'll be making your husband so happy by giving him a boy," as if she'd been put on earth solely to bear her husband an heir. Your comeback is obvious: First count to ten to avoid using profanity (what if your baby's listening?), then say, "My husband would be happy with any baby we had." If you're keeping the baby's sex a secret, gently explain that although we live in frighteningly modern times, you and your husband simply choose to be old-fashioned about such things.

What are you naming him/her? This can be a highly charged question, especially if it comes from a grandparent-to-be. One friend took the tack that nobody, no matter how thick the blood, was to know her infant's name before the birth. "People tend to like the name better and keep their criticisms in check when they're holding a cute baby," she contends. My husband and I decided to share our name with a handful of people, just in case someone had heard that it belonged to, oh, an ax murderer, for example. (One cousin thought there might indeed be a serial killer who bore our son-to-be's name, although a lengthy Internet search couldn't confirm it.)

People will try to guess when you're due. This can be upsetting. For instance, in my fifth month, a lovely young man who works at my office informed me (incorrectly) that I was definitely having twins because I was "so big." Yet one of my friends who'd suffered from acute morning sickness and lost considerable weight early in her pregnancy was extremely unnerved when told she didn't "look" pregnant. Though you'd probably prefer a left hook to a stiff upper lip when confronted with such impertinence, dignity dictates restraint. But it's no lapse of civility to shrug and tell the overly inquisitive that your baby will ultimately decide his own due date.

People will assume you've given up your career. I know that it's the twenty-first century, but I couldn't believe how many people asked me when I was going to stop working. The right thing to do is politely tell the asker that you're sure you'll have to make some adjustments for the baby, but writing/doctoring/banking (fill in the blank) will always be part of your life. In a particularly sensitive moment, though, I actually had words with the doorman when a package from my office was delivered and he assumed it was for my husband. "I know you're upstairs all day long these days, but I didn't think you were *working* up there," he said. I squelched the desire to tell him that our Christmas tips actually come from my salary, not my husband's.

People might feel compelled to tell you baby horror stories. "When she found out I was pregnant, a colleague told me the entire story of how her baby died of SIDS [sudden infant death syndrome]," recounts my friend Cara, who should not under any circumstances have listened to that story. Pregnancy is worrisome enough without people giving you more things to fret about. Gently deflect a person when she starts such a tale, and tell her that you're so sorry for her pain but can't bear to hear such things in your current state.

Expectant mothers can expect other embarrassments, too. People you barely know will rub your stomach, invading your personal space (and one time, getting black ink on my white maternity blouse). Others will lean down and start shouting words of wisdom to the unborn baby (and even though they're the ones who look foolish, it will be you who feels that way). Some will even steal the taxicabs you hail, simply because they can scramble faster than you can. I found that being nice, or at least trying to, in the face of thoughtlessness made me feel better about the world into which I'd be bringing my child.

Ultimately, I realized that for every unpleasant encounter, someone else more than made up for it with an act or word of kindness. I truly enjoyed the Monday-morning pregnancy updates with my dry-cleaner's wife as well as the extra delivery service the grocer and the gourmet takeout gave me. My husband and I grew closer to our best friends, whose due date was seven weeks behind ours— and were more than delighted to share with them the intimate details to which strangers felt entitled.

As I wait, impatiently, for the first sign of labor, I feel compelled to leave you with this one final thought: It can be very nice that people want to get caught up in the happiness of your pregnancy. And if you set the proper boundaries by being polite, if at times firm, sharing the experience might even be immensely pleasurable.

And now I must go get that chocolate-chip cookie.

Whose Wedding Is It, Anyway?

by Susan Dundon

'Bluegrass?"

"Yes, Mom. Bluegrass."

I recognized the tone. It was challenging, without being overtly rude. Silence filled the phone lines while I tried to think, first, of what exactly bluegrass was and, second, whether a woman of my vintage could dance to it. I have enough trouble orchestrating my feet to music that is familiar to me. My prowess hasn't progressed much since my father, helping me prepare for my first dance, box-stepped me around the living room to Al Morgan singing "Jealous Heart," played on a scratchy 78-rpm record.

Bluegrass, indeed. But whose wedding was this, anyway?

Of course, nothing could quite match the joy I felt anticipating this celebration. And yet, as any parent who has planned a wedding can appreciate, it was a time with more than its share of conflicts. Each detail—and I was astonished to learn how many there are in even the simplest affair—presented an opportunity for an intergenerational incident. I worried sometimes that complete alienation was just one heated word away.

Any project that brings together two or three generations is likely to bring with it a clash of values, differences of opinion over what is traditional versus what is in vogue. The trick is to reconcile these differences without wreaking havoc on the relationships in your family. You don't want to make an enemy of your daughter and have her go off on her honeymoon vowing never to see you again.

A generation ago, it was typical for the parents of the bride to plan and pay for the wedding. Most of today's young women, on the other hand, have grown up in a more democratic environment. They have been encouraged to make their own decisions. They would be justifiably infuriated if we were to turn around now and say, "You stay out of this; I'm in charge."

Making matters more complicated is the issue of money. All those independent-minded daughters we've raised might not be as malleable as young women before them when it comes to parents automatically footing the bill. So mothers and fathers may need to emphasize (as I did) that the wedding is a gift.

> Any project that brings together two or three generations is likely to bring with it a clash of values, differences of opinion over what is traditional versus what is in vogue.

Gift or no, it was still tempting to fashion my daughter's big day after my own image—and I did have the loveliest idea of just how it should be! But this was her day. Not that I wasn't reminded of that fact in more than one tight-lipped conversation. The band, let me tell you, was just the beginning.

It helped that during this time we attended the weddings of several of our friends' daughters. I was struck by how different these ceremonies were and how each reflected the personalities of the people being married. One was a magnificent affair with all the traditional trimmings, including eight bridesmaids. I happen to know the parents would have opted for something more understated, but this was exactly what the bride wanted, right down to the purple ribbons used to bind the programs.

Another took place in the bucolic splendor of the bride's family estate. Included among the roughly one hundred and fifty guests were several dairy goats who ambled over to the fence to nod their approval as the couple spoke their vows before a judge, a longtime family friend. Although I'd never seen the bride's parents look happier, there was no question as to whose wedding this was: Even the main course, rigatoni and meatballs, was selected at the insistence of the bride. We can only imagine the familial stir her choices surely caused. At first. Trust me when I say how little it must have mattered as this magical celebration unfolded.

These same friends hosted the wedding of their younger daughter a short time later. True to her individuality and sense of humor, she made her way down the aisle to a single tuba playing the "Wedding March." No doubt there were a few moments of behind-the-scenes dissent in the planning of these festivities. For it to have been otherwise would have been strange, indeed, as if no one cared. But to all those present, it seemed that the ultimate consideration had been given to the happiness of the bridal couple.

As potential adversaries, my daughter and I were lucky. She wanted nothing outrageous, that is, if you don't count her wish to have the family dog present. (In a weakened state, over a glass of wine, I said, "Yes.") On most other matters, there was no dispute. We agreed on the site, an old and beautiful estate in nearby Philadelphia, and that the ceremony should be in the garden. Nor was the number of bridesmaids and groomsmen in dispute. My minimalist of a daughter wanted none. Not wishing to choose among their friends, she and her fiancé elected to have her brother and his sister as witnesses.

Yet to be resolved were the issues of what the invitations would look like and how they would be worded, what everyone would wear, the menu, who would provide the flowers and the cake, whether we would have a sit-down dinner or a buffet (we decided a buffet was more appropriate for this occasion), and this: Mom, do we really have to have a receiving line? (I thought we did but acquiesced when my daughter happily agreed to greet each of her guests personally.)

But despite the conciliatory mood that can make life less stressful over the months of wedding planning, I do think that parents have a right to insist on certain things. These include the size of the wedding and the general atmosphere you wish to create. For my part, a sort of timeless elegance with room for a contemporary twist seemed appropriate. That ambiance seemed at risk when it was suggested to me that we have beer on hand for some of the guests. We were serving Champagne throughout, as well as wine and mixed drinks. That seemed sufficient; I wanted to give my daughter a wedding, not a fraternity party. (Let's just say that I was encouraged to have beer available—no one would be forced to drink it—so I ordered some.)

If you are the hosts, you also ought to be entitled to define what constitutes a "small" wedding. It is not, as some friends have painfully found, two hundred and fifty people. Once the "afterthoughts" start appearing in the guest list's margins, there's no stemming the tide. Sometimes harsh choices must be made, as each faction faces a cut or two. But these can afford moments for both generations to show what they're made of, moments for bonding.

Not everyone is as apt as I am to get into a snit over the invitations. It was important to me that they be worded properly, especially since my daughter's father and I are divorced. In addition, I took a firm, but safe, position with respect to response cards. I was in good company. Miss Manners herself believes that civilized individuals can take the trouble to write a note either accepting the invitation or expressing their regrets. I have seen others solve this problem by enclosing blank, self-addressed note cards, making their return easy while allowing people to compose individual messages. My daughter and I thought this was an acceptable compromise.

A little more gnashing of teeth accompanied our discussion about whether the groom, since the service would be so simple, ought to wear a tuxedo. My daughter, fearing a tuxedo would be tantamount to capital punishment (it was June and the wedding outdoors), prevailed on that one. Her handsome bridegroom wore a dark suit.

Today, I recall with fondness that awkward moment on the telephone with my daughter when my visions of Cole Porter at the piano gave way to a barefoot banjo picker. The next day, in a spirit of détente, I went out and bought some bluegrass tapes. I was not reassured. I certainly didn't think I'd be able to move to what I was hearing. As things developed, I didn't have to. The ultimate choice—of the bride and groom—was reggae. It, too, was a long way from "Jealous Heart," but it was fine. The groom's grandmother certainly had no trouble with it. Surely, the same might have been said for bluegrass.

Yes, bluegrass.

IV
A WORD'S WORTH

Character can be measured by what we say . . .
and what we don't.

Curses!

· by Jonathan Alter ·

y father was a World War II hero who flew death-defying bombing missions over Nazi Germany. Over the years he has admitted that nearly every time his plane took off he was scared sh— well, I can't say exactly how scared he was, for reasons that relate not just to my father but also to my children—and even to World War II. I must confess, though, that I employ that particular phrase rather frequently in conversation, as do most people I know. We come from a generation that all too often uses profanity as a form of punctuation, as if "uh" and "you know" weren't enough.

Language, as George Orwell explained so well, is all about power, and profanity has become a means of ascent. On an almost instinctive level, men and, increasingly, women use it in social settings and the workplace as a shorthand to prove that they are tough, savvy, streetwise. Swearing seems to represent a knowingness and a candor that can equalize (or at least neutralize) certain relationships. Some people even think it can substitute for gutsiness ("I'll tell him off"), as if the confrontational message embedded in profanity had anything to do with real courage.

Women have come to understand that intolerance of profanity, even a red face, makes them appear less likely to fit in. As they made their way into the work force in great numbers during the 1960s, women began to smoke and swear more freely, partly out of habit, partly as a way of showing they could mix it up in a man's world. Now it's considered almost an asset.

In other realms—say, prison—profanity is so common that it almost becomes its own means of communication, conveying disrespect only when used in an especially aggressive tone of voice. The rest of the time it's deployed in the same way other people drop names of mutual acquaintances, as a method of easing social interaction and establishing a sense of community. In the plays of David Mamet, for example, these words are used almost lovingly.

Amid this thickening lingual pollution I'm trying to clean up my own act, and it's not just because I've got kids now. In journalism, words count, which makes it impossible for me to be cavalier about what has put the coarse into American discourse. The words themselves bother me less than the lack of imagination behind them, as if offending people was a function of laziness and the absence of anything else to say.

Profanity is crudeness in the service of supposed sophistication, an effort to convey that one wasn't born yesterday. From Chaucer's *Canterbury Tales* to Martin Luther's *Table Talk*, ribald humor has always found an audience. In fact, we have plenty of evidence that Abraham Lincoln knew how to tell an off-color joke. But Chaucer, Luther and Lincoln used such references to make a point—they were bawdy and earthy rather than profane—and ancestors who swore into their spittoons took care to avoid doing so in mixed company. This wasn't simply about the sexism of the day: Americans used to have a greater sense of place, an understanding that different behavior is appropriate in different contexts.

Today, some of us are feeling more than a little nostalgic for those distinctions. The renewed interest in such authors as Jane

Austen, for instance, reflects not just a thirst for good romance but also a hunger for the comforts of the mannered life. We sense that manners matter and not just for their own sake: They form a protective skin that helps us get along better with other people. That's the idea, anyway.

But sometime in the last half-century or so, the assumption arose that one way to break down social barriers was to break down manners—and swear like a sailor. The pivotal event was World War II, our first war featuring extensive class mixing; one in which John F. Kennedy, the wealthy son of the ambassador to Great Britain, could share a PT boat with a butcher and a truck driver. This was a tremendously positive development that helped to unify the country as never before. And when the rich boys went home to run their fathers' businesses, they had a much more sophisticated sense of the range of human ability.

In journalism, words count, which makes it impossible for me to be cavalier about what has put the coarse into American discourse.

With that awakening, though, came new offensive language. While hardly renouncing the privileges of their backgrounds, the sons of prominent families strove mightily to at least sound more like average Americans. That aristocratic accents faded and a saltier sensibility emerged is clear from reading Benjamin Crowninshield Bradlee's memoir *A Good Life*. The former *Washington Post* editor, who was a close friend of JFK's, is a famously profane man, and that's part of his charm. That's also part of what he and others of his generation left to the rest of us.

As these men grew older, many of the swearwords they used

came almost completely out of the closet. Back in the late 1940s, for example, Norman Mailer used fugging throughout *The Naked and the Dead*; by the late 1970s, however, it was hard to find a contemporary novel that wasn't littered with the real word. While that may have represented a worthy advance for the First Amendment, it didn't do much for the language. The Watergate tapes, full of "expletives deleted," revealed that even the president had a dirty mouth.

Today it's all profanity, all the time. Many magazines use the F word conversationally, reasoning that it reflects the way people really speak. On talk shows from "Today" to "Letterman," it's now common to hear "this sucks" or "that pissed me off" from role models of all kinds; should one of them ever substitute "high dudgeon" or "consternation," I'd fall out of my chair. The word that Barbara Bush said "rhymes with witch" can be heard in prime time.

Young people now swear not so much to be regular guys—long their fathers' and, more recently, their mothers' motivation—but because it is a natural condition of their surroundings. Even the finest schools sometimes sound like the Navy. On the streets, the four-syllable word starting with mother is used as both prefix and suffix. And beyond conveying annoyance, there are times in the moments after a fender bender, for example, when the word can give temporary power to those who feel powerless.

Yet just when American swearwords seemed about to go the way of bloody, the British expletive that moved from verboten to common and relatively inoffensive, something happened: The baby-boom generation started to have children. I remember my brother-in-law once shushing me when I began to swear lightly around his infant. My wife and I vowed then that when we had children, we would figure out a less hypocritical approach. Of course, we haven't. We don't want to completely clean up our own act, returning to the days of gosh and darn. These words ring corny now. Even the pejorative description of swearing itself—cussing—sounds vaguely prudish and unfashionable. But we also got annoyed when our youngsters said butt, and we got more than annoyed when they heard worse at school. We don't swear in front of them, and our friends who have children don't either.

Friends who don't have children are a problem. The trick is to good-naturedly signal them to stop cursing without sounding like Cotton Mather. This works best when done with a sense of humor and a lack of the sanctimoniousness I hear creeping into the voices of some young parents. It's a tough line to walk, and it only gets tougher as the kids get older and quickly discover that one way to share power is to mimic their parents' language—and then watch the reaction.

The largest impediment to breaking through our own mental block about profanity is the assumption that it is a small issue, of interest only to Bible thumpers, grandmothers and politicians who have nothing better to do than try to censor the Internet. But it's only small in isolation. A few swearwords never bothered me much; a few million uttered across the country every minute, repeated to the point at which we become creatures of corrosive habit, scares me sh—. Well, it worries me, anyway. Profanity may not be up there with AIDS or teen pregnancy as a social problem, but it's one of those modern afflictions that eat away at our civility. If we can't be shocked by the ubiquity of profanity, might we at least stay a little offended by it—and strike a blow for a cleaner world?

Put It in Writing

by Helen Gurley Brown

Letter writing. . . is it passé as peanut brittle? Unnecessary as hiccups? I don't think so. Unless your arm is broken and you can't even make an X to sign your name, or you have lost your brains and decided to abandon a seriously efficient form of friend pleasing and friend making, I feel strongly you should be writing letters. I started at age six and never let up. I write dozens of them every week—the old-fashioned way: no faxes or E-mails.

People sometimes tell me they save my letters because they make them feel good. I can't think of a better reason to write personal notes, especially to those who might least expect them: the dry cleaner who got a nasty stain out of the chiffon stole you'd thought ruined, but this genius came through; the plumber who worked in a July heat wave—on a Saturday—to unstall your bored air conditioner.

The late composer Burton Lane was sloshing through junk mail one day, saw a Hearst envelope, figured it was a solicitation of some kind but sliced it open anyway. Surprise, it's me, telling him how much we'd thrilled the night before to Tony Bennett's singing of the Lane and Alan Jay Lerner song "Too Late Now." The composer told me he smiled all day.

Aside from writing smile letters, a letter with a request, particularly to somebody hard to land, can be more effective than telephoning. In writing you can be gracious, persuasive, specific and unnervous, plus the recipient has a chance to think things over. My written requests frequently get what they ask for, so maybe I'm not the worst person to give letter-writing advice. I gave a lot, in fact, in my book *The Writer's Rules*. Here are a few suggestions that I think bear repeating:

- Short is usually better than long, not just for business and asking-for-something letters but for personal ones as well. Does the recipient really want a ten-page account of your trip to the Grand Canyon? Report the news; don't drone. (Do you feel as I do that those endless Christmas tomes are pretty much written to gratify the writer, not the receiver?)

- Type or word-process business letters, of course. The handwritten note may be considered proper for thank-yous, but I haven't written one in years. My handwriting is too hard to read, and typing is faster. The important thing is to do what works for you. People want to hear from you.

- What about your writing style? A good way to start a letter is to ask a question. Takes a little practice to learn to do that, but try openings like "Have you given yourself a hug recently? You deserve one, etc., etc." "When are you going to stop being so generous so I can catch up?" "Did you rent my dinner companion from the U.N.? He knew everything about Sierra Leone." Such openers will grab people's attention. Here's how I began a recent start-with-a-question letter:
  Dear Eduardo: Was there ever a launch party like the one you arranged at the Alcatraz discotheque Wednesday night? I think the answer is no!

- Don't forget about pacing. Some instructors advise using short sentences for most of our output; at least throw in short ones between the long ones. Ernest Hemingway, a Nobel and

Pulitzer Prize–winning genius, was the master of short/pithy. I can't quite go along with Ernest and the short/pithy advisers, though I interrupt long sentences with dashes and dots, put things in parentheses, underscore words to keep sentences alive.

- Write the thank-you *now*. What's needed is your response, not brilliance. You need only thank the way you talk: "Dear Gene, A whole case of Arizona grapefruit. What a neat present!" Or a smidge more detailed: "Sue and I are having grapefruit sliced, juiced, sectioned, left in the shell, baked with Cointreau. It's great to have enough grapefruit for a feeding frenzy." The simplest note will do for flowers or a plant: "The azalea is so beautiful—full of pink blossoms. It's sitting on the coffee table, wowing everybody. Thanks so much."

> The handwritten note may be considered proper for thank-yous, but I haven't written one in years. My handwriting is too hard to read, and typing is faster.

- Send a fan letter. Most of the pleasure of fan letters has to be in the writing; you are moved to get something out of your soul. Be specific about what you liked. Quote a few lines from the play, book or article that impressed you.

- Give a little extra thought to writing a letter expressing your anger. As others have advised, if you write an angry letter, hold it a day or two. Maybe you'll talk yourself out of sending it. Still fuming? Need a wrong righted? You'll be more effective writing calm than angry.

- Watch it a little with "It's so nice you were thinking about me" instead of mentioning the specific present. I've received a few of those "thought that counts" thank-you letters—dead give-aways that the present, possibly a pass-along, was just as tacky as you were afraid it was! Even for a gift you can't be enthusiastic about, try to be gracious. Saying you are actually wearing or using a present is good.

- For the host or hostess, a few specifics are always welcome: "Did you bring the boeuf bourguignon recipe back from Provence? As you may have noticed, I had two Eiffel Tower–size portions." "Thanks for putting me beside Judd Gottschalk. I've always wanted to meet him. Are you a good friend or what!" Tell the party-giver he or she looked great: "Beverly, you were radiant! How did you do that when you had sixteen people to feed . . . sumptuously?" Admire the house or apartment: "What a place! The minute we got home Lydia said, 'We've got to redecorate.'" It's always safe to tell the host or hostess he or she throws the best parties.

Back to you and how you feel on retrieving a personal letter from an envelope instead of accessing the computer. You like it, don't you? As they become increasingly rare, personal notes get more valuable. I want you writing them. No indecision need exist. Will your note seem presumptuous? Will you possibly be considered an ass? Never! You totally can't go wrong writing a friendly (never hateful) letter.

Are you reaching for the pen . . . dusting off the typewriter . . . turning on the word processor? Good! I'm proud of you!

What's in a Name?

by Deirdre McNamer

Crowdedness, in case you haven't noticed, changes manners. Not only has the population of the world increased manyfold during my lifetime, but the *felt* presence of other people has grown in a similarly exponential way.

The technology of contact—cell phones, E-mail, answering machines, faxes and the whispery cacophony of the Internet—has combined with actual population growth to make us literally and psychologically crowded in a way that we could never have imagined just a decade ago. And we all know the implications of that, having watched those poor lab animals in Psychology 101.

In the human world, it seems to me that the feeling of living among growing millions of others has produced alterations in the way we address one another. More nicknames, fewer honorifics, unwarranted endearments. To try to salvage a sense of human intimacy in a quick-contact world, a certain overfamiliarity is setting in.

It must be remembered that our names are important, perhaps now more than ever. They label us; they distinguish us; they present us to others. Before you know much at all about a stranger, you know the stranger's name. Though generally assigned at birth, before much personality is present, a name can in a weird sort of way come to express the essence of its owner. The boy who teased me the most in fourth grade was named Cody Van Heel. The man who saved me from the romantic haplessness of my late twenties is named Bryan Di Salvatore. You'll never convince me that those names are accidents.

In my novel, *My Russian*, the protagonist feels a desperate need to become someone else for a while, to see her life from the perspective of an outsider. The first step she takes in accomplishing this switch is to change her name and to begin accumulating the fake documents that will allow her to officially exist with that new identity.

One's name is one's identity in a certain fundamental sense. That's why it's important to exercise some respect when we address others (just as we would in telling them how we would like to be addressed). Their names are bound up in their sense of themselves, and when we decide to change them to suit *our*selves—via shortened versions, substitutions, first names used too soon, mispronunciations—we are saying, in effect, that we don't care all that much about the self-identity of the person we are naming.

In grade school, a certain nun I will call Sister Agatha of the Thorns decided that my name was no longer Deirdre or Dee, my stated preferences. It was Marydee, one word. Mary is, in fact, my first name, but it is one of those residual fins of a name—a nod to a deceased relative, not meant to be functional. The nun tacked it on because it made me sound more emphatically Christian, and I'm sure she thought that was a friendly thing to do. But I did not choose the new name. Its entire function was to make her, not me, feel more comfortable. And that's a workable definition of bad manners: the failure to imagine, and then act upon, the preferences of others.

My friend Jacqueline tells me that new acquaintances frequently address her as Jackie, though this is an appellation she has never, ever invited. She is simply not a Jackie, though she does have another nickname, and if you come to know her, she expects you to use it. It's quite simple, actually: You just don't alter someone else's name unless you've been invited to do so.

But what constitutes an invitation?

Self-introductions would seem to remove all doubt. "I'm Dee McNamer," I might say to someone I've just met. Clearly, the person has no obligation to use the more formal Deirdre. I've made that clear. But what if the person is much younger than I am, or in a position of less authority? An example: I teach college writing classes. If I introduce myself as Dee McNamer, what should the civilized student call me? Professor McNamer? Ms. McNamer? Deirdre? Dee? It's not exactly clear, so that means I should offer further assistance. "I'm Dee McNamer," I might say. "Call me Dee." If I don't remember to offer a version that's so familiar, the student should probably err on the side of overformality.

What if someone you've known for a long time changes her or his name? Patsy has divorced the cad and now calls herself Patricia. Apostolos's Old-World parents have died and he now wants to be called Art. Turbo has joined a big firm and readopted his given name, Clarence. This one's more difficult because the old name evokes connections and memories and the new one doesn't. Adjusting to the new name can be a strange experience. Do you, the old friend, have an obligation to use it?

In cases like these, straightforwardness is probably the best policy. You ask point-blank: "What would you like me to call you now?" And if you get a dispensation from the new name—which is likely—it's still best to keep Turbo to yourself when you're both among strangers.

A friend's six-year-old child recently requested a private conference with her attorney uncle. They emerged from the kitchen with a piece of paper in language that sounded legal enough to be true. It said her name was no longer Sarah. It was Sparkle-Ann. So convinced was she of the rightness and beauty of this new name that her family was temporarily swept along. "Sparkle-Ann," her brother called out at dinner, as if she stood on a far shore, "please pass the bread." No one could keep it up for long, though, and Sparkle-Ann is now Sarah again, and doesn't seem to mind.

But she will grow older and more powerful, and will take her place in a jostling world where her name will sometimes feel like her best way to say who she is. And if she then takes it into her mind to ask others to address her as Miss Sarah Snow, or to stop addressing her as Sassy or Hon, well, that's her prerogative. It's her name, not ours.

Just Say You're Sorry

by Deborah Tannen

 prominent restaurant critic once explained in an interview that there are certain offenses that doom a restaurant in her eyes, such as not being seated until 8:30 when the reservation is for 8. There is one way, she added, that the restaurant might redeem itself: if the maître d' apologizes and, to give the apology substance, offers something like a complimentary glass of wine.

Apologies are equally powerful at home. I observed this when two friends—a married couple—had a disagreement in my presence. The wife and I were busy making dinner when the husband returned from an errand that had kept him away much of the afternoon. The wife was angry, because he'd agreed in advance to share in the preparations. He explained that he'd surmised his help was not needed when he learned I would be there. To her, the point was not getting the work done; she had looked forward to doing it with him, and he had exempted himself without discussing it with her. He saw her point, and she saw his; yet she was still angry. At this impasse, he offered, "I don't know what to say."

In a gesture of mock secrecy, I raised my hand to hide my lips from his wife and mouthed, "Apologize." "What?" he asked me. This time, I whispered, "Apologize." Still confused, he walked over to me, and I said in a voice loud enough for both to hear, "Apologize!" He laughed out loud. "That never occurred to me," he said. But his wife agreed: "Yes, if you'd just say you're sorry, I'd forget the whole thing."

So he did, and so she did. And so did I observe once more the power of that small conversational act to restore peace.

Why are apologies so palliative, so disarming? And why do so many people resist offering them?

Apologizing entails admitting fault. Many people see this as a sign of weakness that invites further assault. In some cases, that is true. But often the effect is just the opposite: The apology forestalls further attack by allaying the anger of an aggrieved party. Yet despite the nearly magical properties of apologizing, resistance to it persists, in part, I think, because of what I call our "argument culture," which is, in fact, the subject of my book *The Argument Culture: Moving from Debate to Dialogue*. In public discourse all around us, human relationships are modeled on a metaphorical battle between two polarized sides. Television shows and news reports frame issues in this way: Though Westerns have been replaced by plots of crime, intrigue and governmental wrongdoing, the underlying dynamic is like a shootout between two gunslingers, which one must lose while the other wins.

Nowhere in recent history was this made clearer than in the complex and far-reaching developments of Kenneth Starr's investigation of President and Mrs. Clinton, which have been pressed into this familiar script. The saga included President Clinton's much-debated statement of regret to the nation. So we read about victories for Starr or Clinton, or the "showdown" between them, rather than the implications of judicial and political decisions that will affect the country long after these two men have moved on. Against the backdrop of the argument culture, the fear of losing becomes paramount. Apologizing, then, can seem all the more like a defeat.

Reluctance to accept blame is exacerbated in our litigious times by fear of a lawsuit. Let's say you're involved in a minor car accident, and you know you caused it. You'd like to say "I'm sorry," to do what your human inclination urges you to do. But you feel you shouldn't, because insurance companies admonish: "Never admit fault."

Substituting legal procedures for a simple apology can create more frustration rather than less. That point was captured by a caller to a talk show on which I was a guest. "I was recently involved in a legal dispute with a neighbor," she explained. "We've been paid money, but I still feel unresolved because what I really wanted was an apology." Ironically, the caller was an attorney.

Apologies work their magic in myriad ways. Among the most surprising: They can prompt someone else to admit fault. Apologies typically come in pairs and constitute a ritual exchange. I say I'm sorry for X, then you say you're sorry for Y, and we both consider the matter closed. Twin apologies are the verbal equivalent of a handshake. So if I think you are at fault, one way I can get you to apologize is to speak the first mea culpa; this should compel you to do your part and utter the second.

But, as with many social rituals, taking the first step incurs risks. Suppose a friend arrives at a restaurant fifteen minutes late. You get angry, and he feels you're making too much of a small offense. To end the dispute, you say, "I'm sorry I overreacted. I had a bad day." You expect him to say, "That's okay. I'm sorry I was late." But what if he fails to take any responsibility and instead says, "Yes, you did overreact. Try to keep a lid on"? You feel like someone who's climbed onto a seesaw, trusting the other person to keep you aloft only to have him step off and send you crashing to the ground. The argument is likely to be off and running again rather than ended.

In a society that values aggression over conciliation, as ours does, some curious reasoning can take root. This emerged in another call to a radio talk show I was on. A woman recounted the time she was in a waiting room where a man was smoking directly under a No Smoking sign. Instead of saying "Don't you see that sign? Put that out," the caller politely said, "Excuse me, sir. I have asthma, and your smoking makes it hard for me to breathe. Would you mind very much not smoking?" The man graciously obliged. The caller's question to me was "What's wrong with me?" She was expecting me—the communications expert, the linguistics professor—to tell her she should have been more assertive. But the way she handled the situation sounded perfectly fine to me. She got what she wanted without humiliating the smoker. Had she taken a more confrontational approach, he might well have resisted complying or even become belligerent.

The caller's method of getting the man to stop smoking was just a ritual, a socially agreed-upon way of getting what she wanted while saving face for him. After all, that's what getting along in society means. We have many ways of saving face for each other and also getting what we want. That's how communication works. And that also helps explain the power of the seemingly simple but deeply satisfying act of apology.

When Money Squawks

by David Brooks

Some years ago, a business magazine asked me to contribute to a column called "Me and My Money." It was a cream-puff feature in which prominent people were asked about their favorite charities and investment strategies, and I was to do a financial profile of feminist provocateur Camille Paglia. To put it mildly, Ms. Paglia is not allergic to publicity. She's a Roman candle of outrageous personal revelations. But when I asked her to cooperate with this little financial feature, she faxed me back a note saying she couldn't possibly do it: "It's much too personal." After I'd picked my jaw up off the floor, I felt a glow of respect for Ms. Paglia. We live in an age of spectacle and debauchery, but apparently discretion is not totally dead.

It figures that one of our last taboos should be about money. As I tried to describe in my book *Bobos in Paradise: The New Upper Class and How They Got There*, the Information Age has produced a group of wealthy Americans who did not go into adulthood seeking money. But they founded organic ice-cream chains, gourmet-chutney cooperatives and countercultural software firms, and the money found them. Add to this group the "Squawk Box" addicts and all those hair-trigger day-traders and you have a great floating mass of people stumbling through their baby steps in the world of affluence.

The problem is that many of the members of this new class don't always know how to discuss money socially. They aren't sure if they're supposed to brag about their wealth or renounce it to prove they're spiritually pure. And because the rest of us find ourselves brushing up against them at parties and elsewhere, we land in all sorts of awkward situations when the conversation turns to things financial. In the interest of clearing up the social confusion, it might be worth reviewing and updating a few conversational matters related to the M word.

Don't pretend money does not matter. Some folks, especially in Silicon Valley, try to wish the whole business away. "The money doesn't mean anything," the Internet zillionaires will declare. Or they'll say, "It's just a way of keeping score." When you hear someone speaking that way about money, you know that person has enough of it to purchase several small countries.

In general, people who have to spend time worrying about the next mortgage payment don't like to hear anybody tell them that money is insignificant. Nor do they like to hear the self-made successes pretend that getting rich was the furthest thing from their minds. These saintly moguls act as though the money just happened to land on them while they were out pursuing their creative vision of being the Picasso of the home-furnishings industry. (Somehow, it seems, they never get around to describing their efforts to drive the competition into bankruptcy.)

Stay inside the lines. Some topics should be socially out of bounds: salary, house payments, alimony (whether you're the payer or the payee), trust-fund balances. It's acceptable to mention how much you've paid for things everyone can afford, such as socks and movie tickets, but it's not polite to enumerate how much you spent on your luxury box, your second home, your tiara. Should your dinner mate start veering into these areas, it's best to change the subject to the weather before the I've-shown-mine-now-you-show-yours dynamic takes over. (And if anybody desperately wants to know what you paid for your house, force him to look it up on the Internet like everybody else.)

Beware the pry-baby. Yes, you may honor the letter of the above advice, but there now lives a certain breed bent on being totally open and frank about money—yours! Possessing the souls of IRS auditors, they will go to any length to get you to spill the beans about how much you are worth. And you're more likely to be the prey of a pry-baby if you're of a certain age: It's a sad fact of life that after you pass forty, people stop prying into your sex life and start prying into your bank account.

The pry-baby will begin by probing those income streams that he imagines are socially acceptable, i.e., your book advance or stock-option package. Then, often boasting about his own investments, he will move up your consumption ladder: How much did you pay for your car, your vacation, your new kitchen? Enough is enough! Don't be afraid to walk away or, if you have the belly for it, to deliver a little lecture about something that's really gotten to be expensive: privacy.

Learn from history. When it comes to talking about money, the Old Rich have a lot to teach the New Rich. The WASP aristocrats—or at least those who were on their best behavior—never pretended that money didn't matter. But they broached the subject using a dignified code so that it didn't just leap out naked and dominate the conversation. The Old Rich rarely talked about money numerically. It was the quality of money that mattered, not the mere quantity. They would never even use the word rich, certainly not about themselves, though they might say that somebody was in possession of a "considerable" fortune.

The Old Rich even had a sliding scale of euphemisms. Those who might have said they were "well off" didn't need to worry about the grocery bills but probably weren't able to go around endowing museum wings. Someone who said "We've been fortunate" might have, oh, a boat and a place in Newport. "We've been blessed" translated to a string of boats and more places than he could count. Those who were "truly blessed" were in a position to acquire the Cunard Line.

Indeed, if we simply can't resist throwing in our two cents (adjusted for inflation) when the tantalizing subject of money arises, speaking in code may be the best way to maintain some semblance of decorum. Let's see. . . . If your dinner companion lets slip that she'll be "retiring at thirty," it means you can graciously let her pick up the check. If someone complains about how long it takes to read through his shareholder report, he probably deserves a place on your benefit committee. If she looks at you uncomprehendingly when you use the words "phone bill," that's a silent indicator that she has enough staff to take care of life's trivialities.

The important thing is to keep financial talk vague. By doing that, we can place money in the background, like a distant and majestic mountain range. And by talking about money less, we can indulge in the luxury of thinking about it less. And, Old Rich, New Rich or Non-Rich, that's a luxury we would all enjoy.

In Memoriam

――・ **by Jim Brosseau** ・――

I'd sat through a fair number of eulogies in my time, but this was the first one that made me squirm. The well-meaning speaker—a prominent journalist, just as the departed had been—intended only to amuse mourners with an insider's remembrances of his former colleague. But there was nothing funny, the polite titters aside, in the revelation that the subject of this gathering had been rather, shall I say, imaginative with his expense account. What was to have been the evening's much-needed light note cast a pall on the reception line. For many, there was fresh meaning to the requisite "I'm sorry" delivered to the sad, and now embarrassed, widow.

We must have our memorials, whether they take the form of a funeral—generally a religious service which takes place within a few days of death—or that of a gathering, often nonreligious, held several days, weeks or even months after a private interment. But whenever or however these services are conducted, they satisfy an almost primal need in all of us. Through High Masses and, occasionally, low camp, we find our stumbling ways to say good-bye. We've always known what we were looking for in a memorial long before it got a name: closure. Today, there are many roads to that psychic balm.

"Services used to be dictated by the standard Catholic, Jewish or Protestant format," says Bill Hartgrove, of New York's Frank E. Campbell Funeral Chapel. The chapel is sometimes called "the

A WORD'S WORTH   127

society funeral home" for the many social figures who have passed through its doors (front and back) since it opened in 1898. "It's human nature to do only what we're used to doing," says Hartgrove, "and it's hard to let people know that they not only can but should be creating something that also has meaning for themselves." (In that connection, grief counselors maintain that even the bereft parents of a newborn should hold a service.)

Many survivors are, in fact, feeling at greater liberty to fashion individualized tributes: In some instances, the deceased's paintings and furniture have been brought into the funeral home to lend a familial touch to the viewing. One woman's poodle, the love of her life in her final years, was walked to the front pew and seated as an honored guest for its owner's church service. And music—everything from classical to disco—has become the elixir of choice at more and more services. I can't remember the song, but I won't forget how Tony Bennett poured his heart into it at the tribute to cabaret singer Sylvia Syms in

> Through High Masses and, occasionally, low camp, we find our stumbling ways to say good-bye. We've always known what we were looking for in a memorial long before it got a name: closure.

1992. (Musical tributes can sometimes present challenges, as when a saxophonist stood just steps from the casket of a fellow musician and played what had been the dead man's favorite song, "Don't Get Around Much Anymore.")

Just as music has its place at a memorial, humor, too, is a welcome attendee, even at the most traditional of services. A group of comedians once bid adieu to a friend by turning her memorial into a laughfest.

With by-the-book observances giving way to the more personalized sort, some are being enlisted to speak at services once conducted solely by ministers, priests or rabbis. At times the request can present a moral dilemma. One woman puzzled over the right thing to do when asked to deliver the eulogy for an employee, someone who hadn't always been an exemplar of gentlemanly behavior. Her deft solution? To speak of the kindnesses the man's fatal illness had brought out in others. This allowed her to speak from the heart.

As with any other event involving a large number of people, planning can help keep gaffes to a minimum. With that in mind, some families have eschewed opening up the floor, a practice that can invite long-windedness or the sharing of a memory best kept private (like the expense-report trickery).

Perhaps you can determine the bounds of a civilized memorial by asking yourself how you might wish your own to be conducted. Music? Lots of speeches? In a church? An open field? I've left more than a few services saying to myself, I sure hope that doesn't happen at my funeral.

Not even the most strident etiquette advocate would insist that you should leave your loved ones copious notes on your own service. Yet giving them some indication as to what you would like—or, just as important, wouldn't like—can help ensure your wishes will have a fighting chance of being fulfilled. Betty Beale, the legendary Washington society columnist, was attending a funeral many years ago when, as she puts it, "I thought to myself, 'What if I popped off tomorrow?'" Beale went home and outlined for her husband all the things she wanted in her own funeral, including the prayer (an untitled Christian Science verse that begins, "Sense to soul my pathway lies before me") and the music ("Sweet Georgia Brown"). A speaker would be fine, she told her husband, "if you can find anybody with something nice to say about me." (Beale recalled one speech at a Supreme Court justice's service that could have used some editing: "There are certain points in a eulogy when it's the right time to stop, and he passed two of them.")

Maintaining control over one's own memorial may be the logical end game for the age of self-empowerment. Yet no verbal reminders, no meticulous lists in bank vaults can guarantee the crowning bon voyage of your dreams. (The single exception may be the spare 1995 service that social moth Jerome Zipkin demanded and got—but then, even in death, who would have dared defy him?)

It is, after all, the survivors who must call the florist, engage the string quartet, locate that speaker who just might make poetry of loss. Even when strict instructions have been left behind, they still have to weigh their own rightful needs against the desire to please mother, father, son, daughter, friend. As they struggle to find that most delicate balance, at a most difficult time, fairness would dictate that their choices not be judged too harshly.

V
HONOR THY
NEIGHBOR

Some people treat the world as if it were their own living room.
Don't you wish they wouldn't.

Rules for Renovation

by Stephen Henderson

few years ago, on a posh block in East Hampton on New York's Long Island, things suddenly turned nasty. In a flight of renovating fancy, Mr. New-to-town both razed his privet hedge to enhance his ocean view and repainted his house in a vibrant lemon. An outraged neighbor, whom we will call the Yellow Snubmarine, responded ballistically. Overnight, Y.S. planted a hedge of arborvitae on his property so that he might block out the lemon view. It was only after Mr. New-to-town apologetically agreed to repaint his house a less conspicuous color that the green wall came down.

Whatever the nature of a renovation, be it on the grounds of a ten-acre estate or in the foyer of a ten-room apartment, it's bound to test the limits of neighborliness in one way or another. "Renovation is never a normal time," observed New York interior designer Wayne Nathan. "Since it's the most important thing to them, people sometimes forget it's not nearly so to those who live next door." Indeed. Forgetting there is a world outside your four walls is probably the mistake most commonly made in renovation. As America's spending on home improvement hit record levels in recent years, the proverbial welcome wagon driver is now more likely to be sputtering with remodeling rage.

To prevent your dream house or apartment from becoming your neighbor's nightmare, simply recast the golden rule: Renovate unto others as you would have them renovate unto you. Bear in mind, too, that people are inquisitive. A For Sale sign piques some interest, a Sold sign still more, and the posting of a building permit most of all. Unless you live in Wyoming and your nearest neighbor is a hundred miles away, folks will wonder about your plans. So why not just tell them?

Long before work begins, send a note, make a telephone call or pay a visit to the people who live on either side of you (and, in an apartment building, above and below). Brief them on what you have planned. You need not show your neighbors a rendering (co-op boards being an exception) or, unless you plan to colorize the block like Mr. New-to-town, solicit their opinions of your décor-to-be. But a polite apology in advance for any inconvenience your renovation might cause will do wonders. You may even offer to have your neighbors over when the job is done.

Because remodeling is always disruptive, co-op boards, the managing agents of apartment buildings and community associations have long since devised lists of dos and don'ts in hopes of keeping the peace. It's wise to inform yourself about these local guidelines (such as time periods when work is preferred). But respect for your neighbors dictates that you be equally sensitive to a building's or a town's unwritten rules (such as adherence to the prevalent style in landscaping or driveway surfacing). While educating yourself about these details may seem tedious—isn't that why you hired an architect and a decorator?—remember that your neighbors will focus their animosity on you, not on the designers, if anything goes wrong.

Chances are, something will. It's a well-known fact that no matter how carefully you plan, once demolition begins, plans often change. "You push one way in 4A, and something will pop out in 4B," explained Liza Lerner, an interior designer in New York. "No one lives in isolation; everyone eventually runs into everyone else. You don't want bad blood."

Nothing makes blood go bad (or boil) faster than when the renovation of your castle encroaches on someone else's castle. For this reason, whenever possible it's a good idea to hire contractors who have worked in your neighborhood in the past, since they are more likely to know the local sensitivities. In the unfortunate event that something goes seriously awry—your builders trample a neighbor's flower bed or mistakenly puncture a shared wall—stop work on your project immediately and repair the accident first. Such a quick response may well keep any disagreement from escalating.

The key to a neighborly renovation is in anticipating when and where things might become uncomfortable, or unbearable, for others. Preemptive measures are preferable to damage control. So insist that plasterers, painters and other workmen clean up after themselves every day, and make sure that traffic in common areas (such as shared driveways and elevator landings) is disrupted only minimally, if at all. A long job will take more handholding, and a particularly gruesome task—something like installing new windows throughout your apartment— requires an additional request for thy neighbors' indulgence (or enough notice so that they might head to the country early). In

> Preemptive measures are preferable to damage control. So insist that plasterers, painters and other workmen clean up after themselves every day.

fact, keeping your neighbors informed can go a long way toward lessening their frustrations.

Should it be necessary to park a dumpster on the street, make sure it's covered. Birds, other animals or even people can rearrange the contents so that they blow away. The wind, please note, is especially fond of insulation, and just because it's flown free of your property doesn't mean it's not your responsibility.

Not making enemies is good, of course, but if you handle your renovation courteously, it's possible you might even make a friend. When a Manhattan fashion executive I know decided to redo his apartment, he slipped a note with the news to someone he'd never met: the woman who lived next door. She wrote back, volunteering to house some of his furniture temporarily if need be.

Any gesture is better than none at all, and better late than never. Such was the lesson learned by Jennifer Schiff, an L.A. entertainment executive. "We did a major renovation—the works— with a crew in the house every day at 8:00 A.M. for five months," Schiff recalls. "But my husband and I were living two miles away in an apartment, so it didn't dawn on us what a commotion we'd caused until we moved in." So Schiff ordered attractive baskets of muffins and cookies and distributed them to her neighbors. "They said it was the nicest thing anyone had ever done."

In renovation, as in all of life, what goes around comes around. Just when your remastered master bedroom starts to feel comfy as an old shoe, you can count on the apartment next door to come tumbling down. When this happens, remember, to paraphrase the Beatles, the noise you make is equal to the noise you'll take.

The Boor of the Grease Paint
by Wendy Wasserstein

y favorite anecdote about inappropriate audience behavior is one of my own. Well, actually, my behavior was perfect, but the display in front of me was well beyond acceptable limits. We were in final previews for my play *The Heidi Chronicles* at Playwrights Horizons, a prestigious off-Broadway theater. I was sitting in the back row with Daniel Sullivan, the director, notepad in hand, concentrating on the last performance we'd see before the critics arrived.

While Joan Allen was delivering the play's penultimate monologue, a woman just a row in front of me began to file her nails. I still don't know why at that exact moment she felt an urge to do so; perhaps whenever she's moved she reaches for her pumice stone. More likely, she had determined that there was no difference in the expected decorum for watching plays in public than that for viewing "Days of Our Lives" at home.

Thankfully, I resisted my desire to grab her and scream, "You're what's wrong with the American theater." Instead, when the lights came down after the scene I gently tapped her on the shoulder and whispered, "Ma'am, could you kindly put your manicure things away?" I was terrified she'd be polishing in the middle of the curtain call.

Proper behavior is part of any theatergoer's social contract. When I was in eighth grade my class took a school trip to see

The Girl of the Golden West at the Metropolitan Opera. Our teacher advised us to bear in mind that we were ambassadors of our school and therefore must represent ourselves well to both our fellow audience members and the performers. At the time, I snickered, thinking that the singers were certainly not going to spend their time focusing on the impressive ambassadors from the Brooklyn Ethical Culture School. But I was too quick to be snide; I didn't realize then how much any performing artist appreciates, even craves, an attentive and responsive crowd. The joy of a live performance is a kinetic and reciprocal exchange between the artist and the audience. This is true of opera, ballet, recitals, lectures and any other live event (although rock concerts tend to have their own protocol).

Today's casual attitude has fostered other affronts, few more offensive than arriving late for a live performance. Even with ushering policies that keep latecomers from being seated until the first scene or movement is over, stragglers still manage to completely disrupt the proceedings. For a playwright or a choreographer in the wings, not to mention the performers, this is a nightmare. The house chaos inevitably begins just when the work onstage has finally sparked the audience's imagination. It can take several minutes for the performers to recapture full attention.

Winners of the worst-latecomers award are the subscribers to the New York City Ballet at the New York State Theater. This particular theater was designed without aisles interrupting the curve of each row. While this may be aesthetically pleasing, it allows any tardy arrival with a center seat to discombobulate the entire orchestra section.

Once everyone is seated, there comes a more subtle yet still insidiously intolerable distraction: candy. It looks innocent enough, but covered in a cellophane wrapper it becomes mightier than the pen or the sword. Perfectly excellent confections like candy corn (my favorite vegetable) and jelly beans (my favorite legume) are wrapped in a substance that's noisier than a dentist's drill. As far as I'm concerned, sourballs in clear plastic should be banned from the-aters. If folks want to rattle their lemon drops, they should rattle them outside with the smokers. (And, if they're very generous, they could offer the smokers drops to replace cigarettes.)

When candy is banned, the disappearance of coughing, one hopes, won't be far behind. Coughing usu-ally commences just as the lights are going down; curtain-up is almost a "go" signal for phlegm. Personally, I would never have the courage to turn to the hacker beside me and ask, "Now that the first movement has begun, would you mind not coughing?" But midway through a recent concert I thought of donning a small white mask just to give my neighbor a hint.

> The joy of a live performance is a kinetic and recipro-cal exchange between the artist and the audience.

What is incomprehensible to me are the concert halls that pro-vide fishbowls stuffed with cellophane-wrapped lozenges as entrance giveaways. This is practically a neon sign announcing Coughing and Rattling Welcome Here. Isn't it the singers' voices that must be soothed, not the audience's? The audience's job for those few magical hours is to sit back and listen.

The final item in any audience's behavioral contract is applause. The performers—whether they're in the greatest show on earth or in a complete disaster—are generally working very hard and deserve recognition. No taxi is so necessary, no baby-sitter so impatient, no mistress so demanding that an audience member can't wait until after the curtain call to exit the theater. This is not to suggest that you should take your cues from those ballet and opera fanatics who won't let brilliant performers leave the stage, those who are happy to toss bouquets of roses at their idols' feet until dawn.

There are more subtle ways to gauge audience appreciation. I always know if a play of mine is in trouble or doing just fine by listening to the scuttlebutt in the ladies'-room line during intermission. The women in the line, that sisterhood of patience and profundity, never lie. When *The Heidi Chronicles* was at the Doolittle Theater in Los Angeles, I remember overhearing two women discussing Amy Irving's matinée performance.

"You know she didn't have to do this," a lady wearing a purple suit and authoritative accessories said, turning to her friend. "She was married to Steven Spielberg."

"I know," responded the woman in a pants ensemble beside her. "But I think she's wonderful in the play, anyway."

"Yes. She's very talented."

Both ladies were in agreement as the line moved inevitably and gracefully forward.

Yes, for all their lapses, audience members can be not only highly perceptive but also exceedingly well behaved. Most nights, I want to thank every one of them for coming.

When the Tail Wags the Dog

by Marshall de Bruhl

"Mommy's little angel." "Daddy's little girl." Such saccharine effusions aren't used much these days in response to the patter of little bipeds. No, they're more likely directed to a quadruped, *Canis familiaris*, the common dog. To a dog owner, you've perhaps noticed, no dog is common, and no sobriquet too effusive. Excess is the norm, embarrassment unknown. Hamlet's portentous declaration that "Dog will have his day" has come to pass. Canine numbers have grown by leaps and bounds to some 55 million—the largest group of carnivores in the United States.

The triumph of man's best friend was explained by dog collector and animal-welfare activist Frances Hayward: "Dogs are neither four-legged beasts nor pets," she said. "They are four-footed persons." So it's no surprise that at Hayward's estate in the Bahamas, sixteen of the anointed once lolled happily in the main house. She did, however, put them in a kennel when Queen Elizabeth came to lunch. As it turned out, she needn't have bothered.

"Removed? Oh, have they been removed?" Her Majesty inquired. "What a pity."

Truth to tell, dogs can be a joy. I am not immune to their charms. I grew up with a pack of foxhounds and a house dog, and for years I had a vizsla named Zinka, who traced her ancestry back to the Middle Ages in Hungary. No, I have nothing against dogs and the prominence they've come to enjoy in American life. They're not the problem; to rephrase an infamous campaign mantra, "It's the owner, stupid." Dogs generally don't live or walk or travel alone. It's their masters who take them into stores or restaurants where they (the tailed ones, that is) have no business. It's their masters who allow them to foul the sidewalks, trample the flowers, jump on other passengers in elevators and, perhaps worst of all, attend parties.

If you love your friends but cannot find it in your heart to love their dogs as well, it is time to examine what courses of action are available. You can try putting your foot down: "It's either Fifi or me!" But this is risky and must be used very carefully—and never in a house you would miss visiting—because no one in recorded history has ever forsaken man's *best* friend for a *mere* friend. You can also make it a rule to decline all invitations to houses where the dog never hears a discouraging word. Again, this must be reserved for the host who serves only indifferent food and drink.

If you love your friends but cannot find it in your heart to love their dogs as well, it is time to examine what courses of action are available.

Then there's that old standby: allergies. But don't expect this excuse, whether genuine or fabricated, to move your host, not when you consider a recent study showing that barely 20 percent of people with allergic reactions to their pets follow their doctors' advice and get rid of the animals.

Accommodation, some might call it surrender, may be the most viable option. After all, how can one truthfully expect dog owners to acknowledge, much less correct, a problem they can neither see nor imagine? Consider the antismoker who foams at the mouth when someone lights up in the dining room but is delighted when a one-hundred-pound first cousin of the wolf comes to the table. Once the four-legged guest inserts his nose into the action, good judgment flees and the conversation is set. New parents, proud grandparents or recovering patients have to keep their deadening narratives to themselves. The Oscar winner, the Nobel laureate, the Pulitzer recipient must give way as dog owners vie with one another in their anthropomorphic zeal. These are not people with whom reasoned argument goes very far (never mind that it's a truth universally acknowledged that dogs are happier on the floor).

In their rush to ascribe human traits to their pets, owners ignore the fact that dogs can also be rogues, petty crooks and even outright criminals. Human indulgence can lead to real danger. As a New York plastic surgeon reports, each year thousands of people nationally must have reconstructive surgery because Rex sometimes forgets he lives on Main Street and not in the outback.

A most extreme, one hopes unique, example of pathological canine behavior was exhibited by a German shepherd named Lucky Luke, a serial biter once as notorious in the Hamptons as Jack the Ripper. This former street dog was so adept at finding the exposed calf of a noted actress or best-selling author in a crowd of also-rans that his bite became a badge of honor, not unlike a dueling scar from Heidelberg. Lucky Luke's rich diet finally did him in—twenty-seven victims later (lyricist Betty Comden is counted twice). Lucky's owner and each person in her employ saw nothing particularly odd about the dog's ways. Indeed, her housekeeper was heard to wonder, "What did Miss Comden do to upset our Lucky?"

Absent rules of the game and the almost certain failure of sweet reason, what is left for the hounded, those whose worst nightmare is one hundred and one of any kind of dog? What of those who believe that humans, generally speaking, are more interesting than animals, those weary of taking lunch with a Lab or dinner with a Doberman? When all else fails, they still must soldier on, their best weapon a belief that it is not uncivil to expect civility. But let *délicatesse* rule. "Please, I'm on my way to the opera," they could plead, "so I really would prefer that Champ stay down." The more confident might try barking out a few commands—"Sit!" or "Down!" for example. "Roll over!" is not advised: it is an open invitation to mayhem. "Play dead!" might be useful but only if the owner has a really good sense of humor; he may view even harmless instruction as a shocking intrusion comparable to disciplining his children.

Remember, though, that history is on your side: All great movements start small, and murmurs of protest are beginning to be heard. A delicatessen owner tired of a famous diva's dog rummaging among the loaves of fresh bread invoked the public-health code to bar the pesky pooch from his store. His neighbor, a druggist, took more extreme measures to halt the visits to his doorway by a prominent diplomat's pet. After a tabloid photographer obliged the druggist by taking a picture of the animal in flagrante, dog and diplomat found another rest stop. A block away, residents of an apartment building prevailed, at least temporarily, in their fight to restrict canines to the service elevator.

Yes, there are signs that the fair-minded are growing impatient with, ahem, the tail wagging the dog. Could these rumblings of discontent suggest a revolution is at hand? "*Allons mes enfants! Arise! You have nothing to lose but your chiens!*"

Cellular Phonies

by Pearson Marx

Whenever life starts feeling stale, I picture myself speeding along a desert highway, breezily waving at truckers, heading West. This remains the eternal American escape fantasy, so compelling that even a nervous nondriving urbanite like myself embraces it in moments of boredom. In this daydream, however, I do make one concession to modernity: My imaginary convertible comes equipped with a cellular phone. Suppose you run out of gas in the middle of nowhere or a soft-spoken serial killer stops to help you change a tire. Having a cell phone in your car can get you out of a tight spot—and possibly even save your life.

Yet this ersatz lifesaving device can be rife with its own mortal dangers. For example, while everyone knows not to drink and drive, gossiping and driving can be just as lethal. And don't flight attendants routinely have to instruct passengers to turn off electronic gadgets before takeoff? I guess not even the possibility of a plane crash can unglue the garrulous from their cell phones.

In fairness, given that these devices are a relatively recent phenomenon, the rules of protocol governing their use have yet to be formally defined. What courtesy has always boiled down to, however, is a simple awareness of and consideration for those around you. Unfortunately, this is exactly what cell phones interfere with: When you tune in the unseen party on the other end, you tune out those in your presence. (This affront goes beyond the wearing of headphones in public, when—unless you're humming along with your Vivaldi—your lack of sociability is of a passive nature.)

We now ghettoize smokers to the farthest corners of restaurants for fear of secondary smoke; yet secondary babble, though it may not be a health hazard, can be just as irritating. We expect to hear the hum of voices while dining out, but what about when those voices are raised in spirited conversation not across a table but across the airwaves? In just such a setting a friend of mine endured what she has described as an all-time dating low: Her Prince Charmless spent the entire evening taking business calls on his cell phone. "I wish I'd stayed home and watched 'Cops,' " my friend lamented.

No matter where you find yourself these days, there seems to be no escaping the ubiquitous "cellular phony." Shopping in a department store recently, I noticed a woman trying on shoes while she pressed a cell phone to her ear. On vacation, I lay by a pool attempting to enjoy the sun and my book—in vain, thanks to the men shouting stock orders into their phones on the chaise longues flanking me. Once, while crossing a city street, I barely managed to avoid being mowed down by a cell-phone–wielding Rollerblader (as if Rollerbladers themselves weren't menace enough). I have seen people panting into their cellulars at the gym. I have missed easy overheads at set point because my concentration was broken by the chirping of a phone on a neighboring court. Friends have complained about being disturbed by cell phones at the theater, at concerts and even in church!

As long as cellular etiquette remains ambiguous and, therefore, easy for some to ignore, one option is to restrict the use of these phones. Not that this would be any guarantee of privacy. I know a man who bought a cell phone as a way of communicating with his mistress. His wife then hired a private detective, who promptly obtained a printout of every number the husband had dialed from that phone. And when their amorous conversations were tapped and taped, didn't a couple of royal adulterers make the unfortunate discovery that cell phones aren't necessarily secure? (Emma Bovary might have braved this danger; too bad the pertinent technology was still a good century away.)

Despite the risks and other drawbacks, the blanket banning of cell phones would seem a Draconian solution to the problem of their abuse. We can all learn from those paragons of graciousness who are able to take out a phone during a dinner party and avoid giving offense. (Those who aspire to that level of smoothness could start by politely excusing themselves from the room.)

To be sure, cell phones are eminently practical in many situations—timesaving devices that have become a necessity if you live in the fast lane. Recently, however, that lane seems to have gotten rather overcrowded. Once a valuable tool for the truly busy, cell phones now have been embraced as a prop by those who would appear busy. If these gadgets have endured as a status symbol, it is because of what they signify: not just wealth but also success. "All covet something excellent and thereby make it common," wrote the worldly Spanish philosopher Baltasar Gracián more than three hundred years ago.

I remember when it was decidedly uncommon for restaurant patrons to dine and dial at the same time. Growing up, I used to have lunch regularly with my grandfather at Manhattan's '21' Club. Even as a child, I was struck by the solemn deference with which the maître d' would bring a large, black and, above all, silent phone to the table when my grandfather's office called. There was ceremony here, but no display. The stateliness of that image makes today's spectacle of cell-phone chatter in restaurants seem frantic by comparison.

Maybe my friend's date, who spent the evening whispering into his cell phone rather than into her ear, was in the middle of closing a big deal. Or maybe he was just hoping to give that impression. Either way, by taking those phone calls he was making himself seem important. Had he chosen not to take the calls, he would have made my friend feel important, and that has always been the essence of charm and good manners.

Now don't get me wrong: If I ever manage to live out my fantasy of driving to California solo, I will be as grateful for the convenience of my cell phone as for the speediness of my convertible. And yet, I can't imagine breaking the spell of seeing the Rockies by answering my phone, should it ring. Not that I'd be disturbing anybody, of course. But, ironically, by constantly being in touch electronically, we run the risk of being out of touch with our immediate surroundings. Maybe it's not so bad to ignore an occasional mountain peak, but what about ignoring a person? It gives new and sorry meaning to the notion of present company, not included.

What's So Good About Gossip?
—• by **Molly Haskell** •—

ere's a story about friendship and gossip, and the rocky shoals into which those most dangerous bedfellows can lead. I was on my way to a conference when a pal phoned to tell me to be sure to look up a friend of hers, a poet who would also be a conference speaker. We quickly found each other and established an almost immediate rapport.

When I got home, I called my pal to say how terrific her friend was and what a performer she'd been.

There was an ominous silence. "Didn't you notice something odd about her face?" she then asked.

"Well . . . no," I said, feeling as if I'd been put in a bind. I was clearly expected to offer some unflattering remark at the poet's expense. If I failed to do so, I was not making good on what was apparently my part in this transaction. I'm ashamed to say it, but I tried for a compromise with a remark that was just a little catty. I'd hoped to somehow pass through this social Scylla and Charybdis.

It was not to be. Several months later I spotted the poet at a party. Upon seeing me, she turned on her heels and marched conspicuously in the opposite direction.

Oh, gossip! That casual and seemingly innocent social pastime so filled with pleasure, so fraught with peril. Condemned through the ages by moralists ashamed of its prurience and afraid of its power to do evil, it nevertheless remains a crucial part of social intercourse. What would we do without it? But how do we contain its damage? The minute we lend an ear to a slur or a slander we become a party to its spread, for listening is not a passive act.

Some historical periods seem more addicted to gossip than others. The eighteenth century was a golden era (some might say a dark age) of cutthroat conversation and epistolary backbiting. But it is no rival to the present, with its countless means of spreading the word. It's a virtual free-for-all of rumor and speculation out there. The Internet merely extends the boundaries of the utterable and blurs the line between truth and untruth. Further confounding the notion of propriety is the public's insatiable appetite for confessional memoirs, all springing from the late-twentieth-century mandate that made it de rigueur to tell all in the name of frankness, honesty and catharsis.

> What would we do without gossip? But how do we contain its damage?

But in our defense, if we gossip more today, isn't it also because so many of us have been uprooted and, living far from our families and friends, feel a desperate need, as E.M. Forster wrote, to "only connect"? Gossip can offer a connection in a world that is increasingly impersonal, harried and heterogeneous, and whose standards of what is and isn't acceptable seem to be changing faster than we can keep up with them.

Implicitly or explicitly, gossip leads to an examination of values, and, to our comfort, we find that we can still be shocked, still summon up moral outrage over someone's behavior. We can still be relieved that at least we're not that bad. At the same time there's a testing of the self and a challenge to complacency: Through gossip we negotiate our position in the world.

Personally, I don't trust anyone who claims never to gossip. Just as extreme as the compulsive, mean-spirited rumormonger is the pious paragon who purports to be above such things. It's partly that we simply don't believe him or her; schadenfreude, that pinprick of pleasure over another's misery, is human nature. And the need to find out what happened (Did he leave or was he pushed from that job? How did she get pregnant at forty-three?) would seem to be so ordinary an expression of curiosity, so natural a way of sharing news and speculation, that anyone who disdains such exchanges is at the very least a stiff, if not a hypocrite.

The question is how to negotiate this tricky terrain. You don't want to betray your best friend or be the bearer of tidings that will devastate the listener, wreck a marriage or destroy a reputation. And you want to be someone who, even in a society with few boundaries, knows how to respect privacy when the occasion demands it. There are gay people who don't want to be outed; cancer patients who are not ready to announce their condition to the world. Yes, frankness about these things has meant salvation to many who suffered in silence and shame; but there are just as many who have perfectly good reasons for not wanting to go public.

I've known a number of powerful executives who've gone into the hospital to be treated for life-threatening illnesses and managed to conceal it from the world at large, lest their position (and stock in the company) suffer damage. Their assistants said they were on vacation in the Caribbean or on a business trip in Europe. And, amazingly, the world conspired to keep their secret: The friends who knew never let on; those who might be competitors didn't want to win that way. They could imagine themselves in that hospital bed.

Of course, through the years gossip has been associated with women, a notion bolstered by such popular images as the Park Avenue salon in *The Women* (George Cukor's 1939 film adaptation of the Clare Boothe Luce play). Rosalind Russell's sharp nails and sharper tongue shredded the happiness of Norma Shearer through the rumor of her husband's affair. But like so many supposed feminine foibles—cosmetic surgery, vanity in general—gossip has come out of the closet as a universal habit. In her 1985 book *Gossip*, Patricia Meyer Spacks took on the judgmental crowd, including such philosophers as Heidegger and Kierkegaard, who "deny the moral possibilities of trivia."

Today, in many quarters, gossip is a commodity every bit as desirable as a hot stock. But this new legitimacy, if that's what it is, doesn't mean anything goes. I have friends I know to be dangerous—and to whom I therefore tell nothing—and others who are reliably discreet or even judiciously indiscreet. One in particular is a world-class gossip, but she relays her information with such innocent and impartial zest that she's entrusted by friends with all the news that's not fit to print. She dishes up the goods with no malicious distortions, like Lexis-Nexis to her plugged-in pals.

We can only try to emulate her, maintaining a polite detachment, observing certain limits on those occasions when we're in a tête-à-tête . . . listening to a friend's seductive invitation over the telephone . . . whispering to a confidant . . . conferring with voices lowered in a restaurant . . . and we're about to give or receive that exquisite morsel that brings with it an almost erotic thrill. A tender duet conducted with a certain delicacy toward the subject (as you would have done unto you) is surely more satisfying than an evisceration. And it leaves a sweeter aftertaste.

Don't Waste Time

·— by Craig Wilson ·—

I was standing in line at the bank the other day, wishing I had a hard surface on which to drum my fingers. Try to be more patient, I told myself. But that's not easy to do when you see people who, when their business with the teller is finished, stand in place, count their money, put things back into briefcases or handbags, or seemingly plan their dinner menu, totally oblivious to the long line of people behind them. I got to thinking—probably not as poetically at that moment—that if the eyes are the window to the soul, then one's regard for another person's time affords just as clear a picture of someone's true makeup.

One of the most blatant examples of taking up other people's time that I've ever witnessed occurred some years ago while the Historical Society of Saratoga Springs was honoring a native son, humorist Frank Sullivan. In an effort to keep the evening moving, each speaker was asked to limit his remarks to no more than ten minutes. The program was going along nicely until one speaker got to the podium and proceeded to tell seemingly every Frank Sullivan story she knew. She'd been speaking for more than a half-hour when the society's program director felt he had no choice but to ask her to stop. It was mortifying for everyone present.

That speaker would feel right at home today in a world where it seems more and more people are snatching from us one of the most precious commodities we have: our time. Sometimes the perpetrators of this theft have all the time in the world, and their sense of self-involvement leads them to think everybody else does, too. More commonly, though, our time is being eaten up by those who feel that they don't have enough of their own.

Time snatching is not new, of course, but the habit of spilling over into other people's time territory seems to be ubiquitous of late. Given today's personal, social and professional demands, it's a wonder anyone stays even close to an on-time schedule. But too many have seized this new reality, this sense that their time is the only time that counts, as their excuse for all manner of abuses, whether it's dominating a salesclerk, keeping him from helping other customers, or showing up late for a business meeting, disrupting the schedules of everybody in attendance.

Even as life has gotten busier, those on good terms with good form understand that respect for another person's time matters as much today as it ever has. Our overflowing calendars require only that we keep a closer eye on the clock. It isn't just your own embarrassment but also that of your guests to consider when your arriving late for the theater forces everyone to be clumsily seated while the show's in progress. And wouldn't it have been nice if that fellow monopolizing the train-station pay phone (the time you forgot your cell) had bothered to notice he wasn't the only one who needed to make a call?

Some people assume that if their lapses aren't intentional, they're less offensive. Tell that to the three friends who recently met for dinner at a Washington, D.C., restaurant. They were ready to be

> Given today's personal, social and professional demands, it's a wonder anyone stays even close to an on-time schedule.

seated but were told they couldn't be until everyone in the party was present. Twenty minutes later the fourth friend swept in. While it might have occurred to her to phone, she did at least buy the first bottle of wine. The gesture helped put her back in her friends' good graces. But it's a good thing they weren't dining at the restaurant of the moment, where arriving late can mean forfeiting your table.

There may be no greater abuse of other people's time than showing up seriously late for a dinner party. No, you needn't arrive at the very stroke of seven, if that's what was called for on the invitation. But anyone who arrives in the waning moments of cocktails signals indifference toward his host, never mind the other guests. The children? The office? Traffic? Sure, these can be acceptable excuses. But all excuses that invoke boorish self-importance (or is that redundant?) are unacceptable. After all, people who still find ways to stay on schedule understand one of the fundamentals of graciousness: Good manners require good planning.

Dinners, concerts and meetings are one thing, but what about cocktail parties? Guests, of course, are intended to freely show up within the suggested time frame. Still, last-minute gridlock can test the smile muscles of even the most collected host. Those who would be "fashionably late" to telegraph how much they're in demand are telegraphing a lot more than they think.

Yes, we live in hurried, harried times. But that shouldn't stop us from taking a few moments to assess our attitude toward other people's time: allowing a few extra minutes if we're going out during rush hour; keeping our remarks brief if we know our colleague has a tight deadline; or, by all means, making sure we're not late if it's raining and we're meeting a friend on a street corner.

Unless, that is, we're bearing an armful of flowers.

VI
A TOUCH OF
TOLERANCE

*If you could create the perfect person, would he deserve more respect
than the flawed one in the mirror?*

Spiritually Speaking

— • by **Stephen Henderson** • —

While spending a weekend in the country once with some friends, I slipped out to an Episcopal service on Sunday morning while my hosts and the other guests were still asleep. When I returned, everybody was up sipping coffee and deeply into the morning papers. Immediately, I sensed my absence had been discussed. This suspicion was confirmed soon enough.

"What did you learn in church?" Bart asked in the singsong voice adults most often use when addressing toddlers.

"Forty days have passed since Easter," I replied. "The priest spoke about Christ's Ascension."

"Did Jesus float up gradually, like a hot-air balloon, or did he blast off like the space shuttle?" Jane wondered aloud.

Hardly a promising start to an enlightening conversation on spirituality. So, doing what sometimes works best when a religious discussion seems headed nowhere, I answered her question with one of my own: What's for breakfast?

As religious intolerance goes, my friends' sarcasm was no burning at the stake. Nor was it exactly a surprise. Quite frequently, in fact, when someone learns that I go to church or that I have a divinity-school degree it elicits just such ribbing. Why is it, I've often wondered, that the same people who are respectful of differing opinions on everything from sexuality to the stock market dispense with civility when confronted with a leap of faith?

For some, it's probably a belated reaction to having been force-fed a heavy religious diet as children. Others blame religion for perpetuating prejudices and stereotypes, or for acting as a training ground for all manner of fanatics. Then there are those who have found organized religions intolerant of them and their values.

Dale Martin, Ph.D., a Yale University professor of religion, offered yet another explanation: "We live in a culture of doubt. So even though we know religion addresses life's most important questions, deep in our psyches there's a fear that nothing about religious faith can be proved." As a result, Martin says, even those with unformed views on spirituality can become uncomfortable when faced with beliefs that they find foreign.

> As old barriers between what should and should not be discussed socially come tumbling down, many still feel religion should remain a purely private matter.

As old barriers between what should and should not be discussed socially come tumbling down, many still feel religion should remain a purely private matter. Well, yes—and no. America has become a place of unprecedented spiritual heterogeneity. There are Hindus in Houston, Sikhs in San Francisco, Muslims in Minneapolis. Indeed, it seems about the only shared belief most Americans now have is that there are no shared beliefs. It's not surprising that the Rev. Calvin O. Butts, as pastor of the Abyssinian Baptist Church in Harlem, has spoken of the "spirit of audacity" it takes for people of different faiths—or of no institutional faith at all—to live together.

Just how is it possible to live so audaciously? Joan Halifax, a Buddhist teacher and the founder of Upaya, a Santa Fe center for the Zen Peacemaker Order, has offered this response: "I like to operate from a place that isn't stuck in dogma. I try to practice not knowing."

To practice not knowing. The simplicity of this notion is tremendously appealing. It also reminds me of a lesson in spirituality I learned one summer while touring the ancient Greek city of Aphrodisias. Here, I was surprised when one of my companions bowed before a statue of the love goddess. "Do you truly believe in Aphrodite?" I asked Melinda afterward. "No," she replied, "but I want to honor those in the past who did." Fair enough. Instructive, too. For this is how we usually encounter differences in spiritual beliefs, isn't it? We find ourselves strangers in a strange land, be it at a friend's weekend house or sightseeing abroad.

When in Rome, should you venture into a conversation on religion, here are some ways to keep things amiable:

- First of all, relax. Just because people speak of their faith, it doesn't necessarily mean they're seeking converts. So try to avoid becoming defensive.

- When someone you've just met at a party mentions his or her religious affiliation, this only tells you so much. More and more people are experimenting with "salad bar" spirituality, mixing a little of this with some of that. There are, for instance, those who call themselves Jewish Buddhists. Keeping this in mind might prevent you from making a knee-jerk remark you'll later regret.

- It's probably not a good idea to ask a complicated question unless you're willing to endure a complicated answer. Religious teachings (think of those thick volumes by Muhammad, Confucius or Joseph Smith) can be notoriously difficult to summarize.

- Public symbols of one's faith—a yarmulke, say, or a sooty forehead on Ash Wednesday—are not campaign buttons. The wearer is under no obligation to explain their significance to anyone.
- It's best not to ask for proof that somebody's religion is true. Having faith demands exactly that: faith. And if someone mentions that she's an atheist or agnostic, bear in mind that these, too, are belief systems—and can't be proved, either.
- Soul-searching has its place, but so does a nice chat about the weather. If your tablemate becomes too strident in his adherence to—or denunciation of—a particular faith, beware! At that point it's probably best to recall the maxim about the perilous place of religion and politics in social discourse.

If following these guidelines sounds too cumbersome, you can always take comfort in the advice of the Dalai Lama. When asked what the essence of his own spirituality was, he answered with one word: kindness.

Sobering Thoughts

by Debbie Seaman

As I made my way through the lunch crowd at the fashionable Paris bistro, I beheld my bête noire waiting for me at the table. I'm not referring to the elegant Frenchman who was sitting opposite my empty chair. *Au contraire.* It was the uncorked bottle of Pouilly-Fumé nestled in an ice bucket that activated my alarms. Not cognizant of my discomfort, my host reached over and poured me a glass. Even as I protested that I'd prefer a Perrier, he insisted that I had to share the bottle. "*Mais il faut!*" he exclaimed. "But you have to!" And for a few seconds there, mesmerized by the glistening condensation forming on the wineglass, I found myself thinking, "Yes. . . . He's right. . . . I have to. . . ."

It had been just two weeks since my last drink, and although I can't even recall what I said to keep that brandished bottle at bay, I think my host finally decided to humor me the way he might a dieter denying herself a dish of crème brûlée. But a dessert had never caused me to forget what I'd said the night before or to call in sick for work the next day. I am a recovering alcoholic, and that one drink others might deem innocuous would reawaken the disease of alcoholism in me, making the difference between a life of health and happiness and a descent into despair and disintegration.

Today, more than a decade into my recovery, I'm still socially active yet no longer hear siren songs from frosty glasses and bottles. In general, we Americans are far more enlightened about alcoholism than we were, say, a generation ago—and indubitably more evolved than the French, who in utter earnestness will declare, "It's only wine!" Nevertheless, I remain surprised at how otherwise savvy people can—more often than not, unwittingly—make social situations awkward for those of us in recovery. Lapses in thoughtfulness usually occur in subtle ways. There's the person, for example, who asks me to hold her cocktail while she dashes off to the ladies' room. Or the guest sitting across the table who looks askance when I pass up the wine and wants to know why. When I reply that alcohol doesn't agree with me, he persists in his probe, asking bluntly, "Did you ever drink?"

Now, I am very proud of my recovery and what I've achieved because of it. Yet I'm reluctant to disclose my status

> I remain surprised at how otherwise savvy people can—more often than not, unwittingly—make social situations awkward for those of us in recovery.

as a recovering alcoholic in social settings, because I've found it often makes others ill at ease. My friend Bob concurs. He'll never forget the time that every person at the table blanched and fell silent when his host at a black-tie dinner, noticing that Bob hadn't touched his sherry-laced lobster bisque, announced that Bob was "one of those alcoholics." When Bob told me that story, we couldn't help remarking on how ironic it is that the same people who give us the odd look might smile indulgently at Harry over there on the sofa slurring his way through another joke.

Some alcoholics are delighted to discuss their past with strangers and casual acquaintances. But it's best to consider it a private matter until the alcoholic himself broaches the subject. So

I'm always appreciative of the host or fellow guest who takes his or her cue from my reticence. They're the same people who know better than to ask, as the potato-chip ad once did, Why I can't have "just one"—or why I'm not "cured" because I haven't had a drink in so long.

I also appreciate the things considerate hosts do that others wouldn't necessarily notice. Because I've lost count of the times I've had to toast with an empty water glass, it's heartwarming when the person pouring the wine or the Champagne at dinner notes my abstinence and stops to ask me discreetly what I would like instead. I'm truly impressed when the trays being passed among guests at a reception or a cocktail party carry nonalcoholic drinks like sparkling water along with the inevitable white wines or mimosas.

I'm equally thankful when someone makes sure that the lime sorbet I'm served does not have the shot of vodka that fortifies everyone else's or when my host asks me in advance whether I mind eating dishes that have been cooked with wine. My own stance is that I don't mind biting into something that doesn't have a bite itself. So, although I won't balk at a *boeuf bourguignon*, I'll hope that, in the event that the dessert is a *baba au rhum*, the host has a tray of cookies on the table so I can indulge my sweet tooth along with everyone else (and not appear antisocial). A sober friend and I, served complimentary *pruneaux a l'Armagnac* between courses at a French restaurant, had a good chuckle when we contemplated how humiliating it might be to fess up to relapsing on prunes. On a more serious note, it is an individual's call as to whether he or she will eat anything with alcohol in it.

Being considerate of a sober friend doesn't necessarily mean donning kid gloves. Just as they would like people not to make an issue of their abstinence, recovering alcoholics generally do not want their friends or new acquaintances to be self-conscious about having a drink or two around them. When I'm going out to a restaurant with a group of people, I expect that some or all of the others might drink. I'll even laugh along with everyone else if a guest regales us with bacchanalian "war stories"—Lord knows, those of us in recovery have many to tell. If a recovering alcoholic is uncomfortable around people who drink (which is most true of a newly sober person), he or she should restrict social activities until, with time, a table covered with glasses becomes merely a backdrop instead of an obsession.

One sober friend encountered a different kind of problem the night she accompanied her husband to a business dinner. As a woman at the table ordered a mineral water, she turned to my friend and confided, "I hate doing that—everyone thinks I'm a recovering alcoholic!" I had a couple of reactions when I heard this tale. First, I wondered with amusement if the woman would have preferred the others to suspect she was a practicing alcoholic. Then I marveled once more at how some people seem to think that life for recovering alcoholics is by definition unhappy or dull.

I had my first brush with this attitude when I was on a vacation about a year into my sobriety. A fellow houseguest decided to mix rum with the fresh strawberry nectar she'd just brought back from town. Her fiancé looked at me mournfully and said, "Too bad you don't drink anymore, huh?" (Talk about inappropriate remarks!) "No, it's not too bad," I replied, politely but firmly. I haven't been handed a life sentence but have been liberated from one, free to lead a life in which I'm capable of doing the best I can.

That's a lot to toss away for a drink.

Political Stomping
.• by Peggy Noonan •.

I was having lunch with five women who've been friends for, at the longest, twenty years and, at the shortest, seven; who know each other and, who, I think, love each other. We were, as occasionally happens when we get together, talking politics, and someone brought up a bill being debated in Washington on a controversial abortion procedure. One woman briefly held forth on her opinion, and all but I nodded in agreement. I held an opposing view, and said why. A discussion ensued; all joined in, I, in time, ardently, and the woman, in time, with some edge. She seemed indignant that, in this nice group of friends, her position would be countered.

We went on for a few minutes. And then . . . silence settled upon us like a fine layer of dust. I was unhappy because I consider conflict embarrassing unless accompanied by the cues of goodwill: the smile, the nod, the "I know how you feel. . . ."

Dessert came. We would refind our old unity in the shared appreciation of cookies on a fine china plate. But suddenly I saw, peripherally, a white and beige object zooming straight at my head. I flinched. It stopped an inch from my nose.

"Want this?" snapped the edgy woman as she held the plate. It was the first time I'd ever almost been hit in a nice restaurant. Weeks later the two of us talked about it. "I was very angry," she explained. Oh, then by all means, do hit me in the head with a plate. Rub the cookies in my hair if that'll help. She was angry because she considers the issue so crucial. I said I do, too, but that even given the depth of my convictions, it would probably be immature of me to conk her on the head. We talked some more, we started to laugh, our anger disappeared.

But what happened stays with me. I think of it whenever I think of what politics can do to nice people, for the woman is nice. She just had a bad moment. But it's a moment I see happening more and more to intelligent people. I am not speaking specifically of a new round of incivility in political discourse. There's always a new round of incivility, because Americans have a long tradition of verbal fisticuffs when we talk politics, and I'm not sure that's so bad. We were founded on disagreement; our national conversation was shaped by the rough to-and-fro of a frontier democracy full of spiky skeptics, an industrialized democracy full of kitchen-table pundits, a technological democracy with a quarter-billion opinion leaders yelling back at the guest on MSNBC. This is the venting of a vast democracy. It's helped keep us stable, and anyway it was inevitable: America was never a place of wholly shared values. The temperance-loving Philadelphia schoolmarms had little in common with the agnostic Jeremiah Johnsons of the West.

Still, we always found a way to disagree, often with a certain vigor, a vividness. It wasn't always civil, but that was to be expected, for these were people arguing, not angels.

Unlike that old incivility, what I'm seeing today is a new smugness. It carries with it a constant justification for bad behavior in discourse that says, "I can be babyishly aggressive, because you are being a bad person by disagreeing with me." It is in its effects the opposite of the old incivility, for the old incivility said, "Oh, you disagree with me. Good, we'll have a great argument." The new smugness, with its unsettling resemblance to Puritanism, says, "You disagree with me? Then you are morally lacking. I am therefore justified in doing what I can to silence you." It is aimed not at rigorous debate but at squelching debate.

When do we see this new smugness? Not just when the subject is abortion, but a host of other issues: affirmative action, gay rights, immigration, Proposition Whatever. These, and more, are seen not as political issues that have a clear moral component but as moral issues that unfortunately have to be played out on the vulgar field of politics. And so to be wrong on these issues—and wrong is defined, in the land of the smug, as holding to views at odds with one's own—is to reveal oneself as not only empty-headed but empty-hearted. As insensitive. And what do we do with the insensitive? We argue not to the issue but to *them*. And if that won't work, well, have some cookies.

You might think the poster child for the new smugness would be someone like James Carville. When I see him on TV I say, "Put up the sound." I know his act will make me laugh, and I know he knows it's an act (the way G. Gordon Liddy, with his hand in the flame, was an act). Carville means it, but he's entertaining us while he means it. It is a generous impulse to entertain, so I give him a pass. The primary reason Carville isn't terrible is that he's ashamed. He knows he shouldn't say what he says. When Mary Matalin shows up beside him on TV and gives him a verbal slap, he hangs his head like the dog that stole the bone. The truly smug never feel shame. It's a hallmark of theirs.

How did this all happen? How did so many people get so politically smug? Part of the answer, I think, is that in the twentieth century, certainly in the latter half of it, politics came to eclipse all other forces. It became more important than class, or region, or even religion. You might say that politics became a religion for a lot of people. When that happens, political views become so high-stakes, so important, that they seem like a declaration of your deepest self, your truest character. We all try to think of ourselves as good, and it's a small leap from there to seeing your political beliefs as an emanation of your goodness. It's another small leap from that to thinking the guy with the "wrong" views on, say, affirmative action is showing his badness. And if he's bad, you could treat him like . . . well, you could put him in the stocks.

What is lost in the new smugness? When people display it, they're saying, in that tired but useful phrase, Don't go there. Don't hold that view, have that opinion, argue that side. What happens when you don't go there? For one thing, you never learn what the other side really thinks, or feels. You never get to change your mind either, because most of us only change when confronted with new information, and smug people don't have information, they have attitude.

> The new smugness, with its unsettling resemblance to Puritanism, says, "You disagree with me? Then you are morally lacking. I am therefore justified in doing what I can to silence you."

Worse, people start to censor themselves to avoid tension and rancor. Debate dissipates, but it isn't replaced by unity; it's replaced by silence, and simmering.

And tossed plates.

The Measure of a Woman

by Véronique Vienne

I had the pleasure of lunching recently with three adorable men, two of whom were wearing bow ties. This being the new millennium, they were on a diet. This being the new millennium, I wasn't. I long ago stopped trying to blackmail my body out of its natural shape. When the waiter asked if we'd like drinks, there was an ominous silence. "Have a martini," said one of my companions. "We don't drink anymore—have one for all of us." The others confirmed that I would be today's designated drinker (and the only one allowed full freedom to order as I pleased). "No olives," I said, sealing my fate. Suddenly, I had a mission: to bring back, just for a couple of hours, an earlier time, a time when women were proud to be girls with curves—and men were smart enough to appreciate them.

This sort of time travel was a simple stretch, comparatively speaking; I've often been told that I was born in the wrong century. That's a nice way of saying I have the kind of body that can fill a big taffeta gown. It's not that I am overweight (well, I could stand to lose a pound or two), but today, few designers cut clothes for women like me: My figure requires too many pleats, darts and seams. Left in limbo between sizes twelve and fourteen, I have no clearly defined shape identity. Words used to describe me run from "voluptuous" and "stacked" to "full-figured" and "big-boned." Some 35 percent of American women are said to fall into that same amorphous category, which means that something as vital as their self-image is at times determined by other people's ability to grapple with hyphenated words.

Whenever someone says to me, "You look great—have you lost weight?" I feel both flattered and frustrated. Yes, I'm glad to look great (a new haircut usually prompts the comment); but why do people assume that I want to be smaller? Compliments related to my size trigger insecurities from my childhood. Suddenly I'm back in sixth grade—a 5'8", twelve-year-old Paul Bunyan in a skirt. Only now, I'm being quizzed about the latest diet or fitness craze.

Funny how, with just a couple of words, a large person like me can be made to feel rather small, my self-confidence shrunk to a petite size four. Backhanded compliments like "You look very healthy!" or "You have such a pretty face" can give a psychological advantage to slighter, leaner people. Maybe that's the way it should be: It's only fair that zero-body-fat individuals occasionally get a chance to throw their weight around. If they didn't, we brontosauruses would probably rule the world! Seriously, though, I worry that our national antipathy toward fat may be preventing some of us from appreciating the beauty of full-figured women: Were Jane Russell in her prime today, would she even be considered for a juicy female lead?

If you fit nicely into a size six and can just about ease a napkin ring around your wrist, take care not to inadvertently marginalize your classically proportioned friends with high-octane, albeit well-meaning, compliments. "I get a lot of enthusiastic comments on my stylish haircut from both men and women," says a curvy friend who looks best when her weight is at its peak. "People also mention my 'presence' a lot, or they say that I look 'taller.' It's always a little trite, and I wish friends didn't feel obliged to say something nice to me. One of the best compliments I ever got was actually somewhat negative: 'You sure don't look frumpy!' a fellow said on our first date. I don't know what he expected, but his candor, at least, made me feel like a million dollars."

For a professional opinion on what women of a certain size want to hear about their appearance, I turned to Saks Fifth Avenue's Beau James, who'd worked in the plus-size couture field for more than thirty-five years. "There are only two adjectives that work: glamorous and elegant," James said. "Everything else is condescending. What women really want is solid advice. My customers trust me because I say No: no to shapeless clothes, no to tent dresses, no to all-black outfits. They trust my compliments, because they know I'm honest with them."

> Whenever someone says to me, "You look great—have you lost weight?" I feel both flattered and frustrated.

But honesty requires you to pay attention. A remark like "Love that color on you!" or breezy queries like "Where did you get that great dress?" may come from the heart. But they never quite do the job, because they feel evasive. I would love to hear someone say, for example, that the youthful austerity of a Jil Sander-like suit "would look fabulous on you." Or something like, "I'd kill for curves like yours."

"No matter how beautiful, thin or sexy they are, women always complain about feeling bloated or big," maintains Joan Weinstein, founder of Ultimo. Her fashion boutiques are refined sanctums for style-conscious shoppers of all proportions. "My customers talk about size more than anything else—more than sex and more than fashion," she explains. "I have never met a woman who wasn't critical of her size."

Insecurity compels some women to pick on people bigger than they are. Once my older sister, a petite as slim as a reed, insisted I try on her old maternity dresses. The funny little trapeze frocks looked like dolls' clothes on me. "This has got to fit you!" she exclaimed at last, taking out of her closet a miniature floaty chiffon muumuu. I couldn't help thinking that some of this familial vaudeville was related to Florence's need to prove that even though she was only half my size, she was still my big sister. For that reason—and that reason alone—I indulged her and watched in the mirror as she struggled to zip me up. She looked as happy then as she did when we were kids and she helped me into my school uniform in the morning. "You are too fat," she said triumphantly. Truth be told, she looked so waiflike, I was glad I could, for an instant, restore her dominance over me. It was a sweetly transcendent moment.

I had another of those moments during that luncheon with my three gentlemen friends. Yes, it took a midday martini and three thousand calories—one thousand from a single slice of *gâteau Saint-Honoré* topped with whipped cream—for me to fulfill my promise to them. But when, sated, I touched my napkin to my lips, the very proper chap sitting across from me sighed: "Now, that's someone you'd want to take on a date." I knew that I was due for a splitting headache, but so what. It was a small price to pay for the look on his face.

Straight from the Heart

by Lauren Picker

he first time it happened, I was at a party. A fellow guest was oohing and aahing over my three-week-old baby, admiring her delicate beauty, her surprising shock of hair, as shiny and black as patent leather. Then she noticed my daughter's left hand, which had not fully developed in utero. The woman looked at me, her face positively ashen. Without saying another word, she scuttled away into the crowd.

By the time Livia was fifteen months old and a new playground acquaintance casually asked me what drugs I'd taken during my pregnancy to cause my child's hand malformation, I thought I'd become inured to these kinds of reactions. I hadn't and still haven't. Every one of them sends me reeling. Not because I'm being held in judgment, but because they are a window onto the kind of reactions I fear my daughter will have to contend with throughout her life.

For the record, I did not take drugs during my pregnancy. Indeed, I was as surprised as the woman at the party to discover that a mysterious developmental mishap had affected my newborn's left hand long before she could even think to suck her thumb. Now she has an extremity that is small, as if clenched in a fist, with a rudimentary thumb and forefinger; from a particular angle, it looks like a doll-size mitten.

My daughter's hand was not the only thing affected by that inexplicable glitch. So were my own perceptions of those I once categorized as "disabled." As Livia's mother, I've gotten an intensive, remedial course in a taboo subject: how to respond when your path intersects, if only briefly, with that of someone who is physically or mentally challenged in ways minute or monumental, someone who is *different*.

I often wish, as any good parent does, that I could be my daughter's guardian angel, shielding her from insensitivity and controlling the words people use to describe her hand. I know I can't protect Livia forever. I am reminded of this with a terrible catch in my throat when I watch as another child inevitably avoids reaching out to her during ring-around-the-rosey. And I realize that when people notice a difference, be it my daughter's or someone else's, they often don't know what, if anything, to do or say. There are no simple answers, but that's no excuse not to pause for a moment and make the effort to try to get things right.

I happen to think Livia's left hand is as adorable as the rest of her, but I realize that seeing it for the first time can be disconcerting. Nonetheless, noticing a difference doesn't automatically give you license to comment on it. Though some people—I hope my daughter will be one of them—are completely comfortable with the topic, many within the psychological community say that when in doubt, it's generally best to respect a person's privacy. "Unless there's a reason that you need to talk about the disability or make some accommodation to it, you shouldn't," contends Nancy B. Miller, Ph.D., M.S.W., a psychotherapist and the coauthor of *Everybody's Different: Understanding and Changing Our Reactions to Disabilities*.

While saying something may ease your own discomfort, it's important to think about the impact of your words. I am very matter-of-fact about my daughter's hand; I don't want her to think of it as a terrible thing to be hidden away. But, if strangers feel compelled to inquire, I prefer that they not do so within earshot of Livia. My fear is that the message will come through, despite my best efforts to teach her otherwise, that there's something "wrong" with her hand; therefore, there's something wrong with her. Similarly, an adult with, say, a prosthetic leg doesn't want attention called to it, even when that attention is intended to be flattering. Applauding the woman who is doing her marketing in a wheelchair, for example, isn't just invasive, it's insulting. As Nancy Miller points out, you may see the wheelchair as a problem when, for that woman, it's simply a solution to a problem.

What hurts is the assumption that a person with a physical or emotional challenge is somehow in need of protection. While that may be the case for some, it is not an intrinsic truth for all. Perhaps it is this assumption of frailty, coupled with the fact that most of us have been raised to believe that staring is rude, that prompts so many of us to look away when we see a man in leg braces proceeding slowly down the street.

This is not to suggest that physical and emotional challenges always ought to go unacknowledged. Holding the door open for a blind man recognizes his disability in a way that satisfies his needs. "I like it when people say, in a considerate way, 'Let me help you,' as opposed to just staring or looking away," noted Cara Egan, a Silver Spring, Maryland, editor with dwarfism (the term she uses to describe her condition, formally known as achondroplasia). Similarly, if a woman in a neck brace jokes that a flight delay is "a pain in the neck," that might be your invitation to make an inquiry about the brace and how she was injured. As with all matters of smooth social interaction, cues and context are everything.

At first, I found it distressing when, in the weeks after Livia's birth, friends avoided the subject that had loomed so large for my husband and me. "Why don't they say anything?" I'd ask. Then, a few months later, I ran into an old friend who'd recently been hospitalized for depression. I wanted to know how he was doing—really doing. But because we were the kind of casual friends who were more likely to share a tub of popcorn at the movies than the darker recesses of our lives, I was afraid he'd think I was being intrusive. Instead, I asked about other things, skirting the question that hung in the air between us.

Afterward, it occurred to me that I had been as unintentionally insensitive as the friends who never acknowledged the emotional turmoil my husband and I were going through. I could simply have asked him, with all the sincerity I felt in my heart, "How are you?" If he'd wanted to pick up the opening, he could have. But even if he didn't, I would have communicated my concern. As Marla Stern, a New York City pediatrician who was born with an arm that ends at her elbow, observed: "The silence is sometimes more hurtful than the actual question."

It's important to remember that just as what you say—or don't say—matters, so does the way in which you say it. As a writer, I thought I'd understood the weight of words. Then, in the hospital after my baby's birth, I asked the pediatrician about Livia's "bad hand" as you might, say, a bum knee. The doctor quickly suggested that I come up with a less negative term; I still cringe at the memory of my blunder, but I'm grateful, too, that someone called it to my attention.

Now, I make a point of referring to Livia's "little" or "small" hand. And not just because it's politically correct but because it's emotionally so. To call an epileptic seizure a "fit" summons images of somebody thrashing about and foaming at the mouth. Calling a person with dwarfism just that or, alternatively, a person of short stature, may be cumbersome, but the term is descriptive rather than reductively defining. The words deformity and even birth defect suggest—to me, anyway—something ugly or Other; difference doesn't have that negative charge.

Minding your language has always been a sign of respect, a quality sometimes overshadowed by pity. Just because a person requires a wheelchair doesn't mean her life is lacking in richness or meaning. To know Livia is to know that her hand may be different, but she is really just the same as you and me. I sometimes wish I could knock on every person's door to tell him that, to introduce him to my smart, lively, perfectly perfect little girl, knowing that his perceptions will be forever altered. Consider this essay that knock.

Fish Out of Water

by Charles Dubow

I had a cousin from a once-prominent New York family who was a classic eccentric. People would encounter him strolling down Fifth Avenue in the middle of a howling blizzard wearing Bermuda shorts and a straw hat. Doubtless, they would shake their heads and say to friends, "There goes poor old Langdon. It really is too bad about him." Tall, good-looking and said to have had "a good war," he had enough money to forgo the pretense of working and was free to indulge his eccentricities to the hilt. He would monopolize the telephone at the Harvard Club's squash courts, claiming to be advising his old classmate Jack Kennedy on his run for the White House. When he wasn't dabbling in politics, he was crashing debutante balls—well into his sixties. Yes, old cousin Langdon was a character—a little screwy, maybe, but essentially harmless.

Many eccentrics can be lumped into the same category as Langdon. They exhibit certain mannerisms or patterns of behavior that society at large regards as oddly amusing if not downright strange. By their nonconformity, eccentrics reinforce our own sense of normality and help us to see the world in a different light. Their idiosyncrasies can seduce us. Who doesn't have a favorite friend or relative whose eccentricities make otherwise dull parties or family gatherings more fun and memorable? I know a retired major of the Grenadier Guards, for example, who likes to liven up dinners at his home by wearing his bearskin at the table.

It's hard to resist the frisson of a little added theatricality to everyday life. Certainly, a monologue delivered by the late Quentin Crisp, the famously flamboyant author of *The Naked Civil Servant*, was likely to be far more remarkable than an explanation of postal codes from an actual civil servant. Yet, as with the movies, when in the presence of eccentrics we are more comfortable as members of the audience. It's all very well for someone else to wear funny hats or talk to the shrubbery, but our own sense of propriety is likely to prevent us from following suit.

> By their nonconformity, eccentrics reinforce our own sense of normality and help us to see the world in a different light. Their idiosyncrasies can seduce us.

While it's easy enough to be entertained by eccentrics, sometimes we have no idea just how to respond to them. The British tend to be better at this than Americans are, but, after all, they've had to be because of their long history and dynastic attitude toward marriage. In fact, the eccentric has become as recognizably British as Big Ben. Still, whether one is British or American, certain things are simply impermissible: Skating near the limits of allowable behavior is one thing; crossing the line is something else.

The dilemma lies in telling where that line is and knowing when it's been crossed. When a man from a socially prominent family was charged with murder in the mid 1990s, it offered a tragic illustration of society allowing a seriously troubled person to hide behind the innocuous description of "eccentric." Largely because of his wealth and family name, people tolerated his strange though increasingly irrational behavior. By brushing aside his outbursts as mere eccentricities and, more important, by displaying an unwillingness to acknowledge the severity of his imbalance, those around him, it can be argued, were partly responsible for his worsening condition. The fact is that he was no longer an eccentric but a sadly disturbed human being.

Americans have become so fearful of offending someone else's sensibilities that we have almost lost the ability to discern what is acceptable within polite society and when to call the police. Dress and comportment that once would have sent the maid running for the smelling salts are now widely accepted, if not actively encouraged. During less permissive periods in history, however, eccentrics were all the more noticeable for their ability to flout society's conventions.

The nineteenth-century English eccentric Sir Tatton Sykes was a mild man, but he found the sight of flowers so distasteful he carried around a cane to lop off the head of any unlucky buttercup or primrose in his path. Lytton Strachey, author of *Eminent Victorians*, was unable to sleep unless he lay under a sufficient weight of blankets; he was even known to drag carpets onto the bed to help him in his slumbers. But eccentricity is hardly a masculine preserve: Peggy Guggenheim's fondness for bizarre eyewear and Congresswoman Millicent Fenwick's predilection for pipe smoking ensured that they always stood out in a crowd. For a more recent example, there's Marylou Whitney's dogsledding adventures in Alaska—proof that when done with enough panache, original behavior does not necessarily tarnish personal style (especially if one is wearing designer mukluks).

It's easiest to define eccentricity by what it is not. It is not a mania. Kleptomaniacs and pyromaniacs may be utterly charming, but they are also very ill and ought to be kept away from shiny baubles and matches, respectively. By definition, alcoholics are not eccentrics. Nor, for that matter, are criminals, vegetarians or Scientologists. Some might say that artists, who frequently have their own ideas about how to live, fall into a special category. Marcel Proust may have had a cork-lined bedroom in his apartment, but then again he did write *Remembrance of Things Past*. We all know people who, perhaps because they think their own personalities flat, affect certain outrageous mannerisms in the hope that the rest of us will find them more interesting. We don't, of course. We find them irritating.

Certainly, eccentricity can be used to mask all sorts of sins. People who are rude, sexist, racist or just plain cheap may disingenuously cultivate a reputation for eccentricity in order to conceal their lack of good manners. A woman I know was staying at the castle of an elderly Scottish laird who awoke her by barging into her room, yanking back the covers, slapping her bottom and bellowing, "Up ye go, lass! Breakfast's on the table!" When the young lady, who customarily sleeps in the nude, mentioned her Caledonian wake-up call later to friends, they laughed and said her host was only being eccentric. I am not as *au fait* about Highland mores as I'd like to be, but it strikes me that the old laird was actually more of an old lecher.

Genuine eccentrics are seldom aware of their unconventionality and, consequently, rarely mean to give offense (a Texas socialite who serves guests leftovers on paper plates comes to mind). When they do, however, it may be best to employ an Olympian sang-froid, knowing it's unlikely that anything we say will have much impact. Yet at other times, there's no alternative but to take some course of action. Those who blithely make racial slurs or sexist remarks ought to be told—politely—that being an eccentric is no excuse for being a jerk. I know of a dowager who always told her relations they were "too fat" or had "appalling taste in clothes." For years they endured criticisms that regularly sent some poor, overweight granddaughter running from the room in tears. "It's for their own good," the dowager would insist with a shrug. Finally, several of her grandchildren banded together and told her that unless she stopped her faultfinding they would cease talking to her. The woman was truly stunned to learn that her comments had not been appreciated, and she agreed to curtail them.

Although the old-money gene pools that once engendered eccentricity are becoming increasingly anomalous in the modern world, I suspect eccentrics will always roam their town houses on Beacon Hill, their villas in Tuscany and their Schlösser in Austria. If their distinctive wardrobes make us chuckle or surprising pronouncements make us think, we are all so much the better for their presence, that is, if we are still able to spot them. The problem is that today everyone seems so strange.

Widow's Pique

by Charlotte Y. Salisbury

When I was growing up back in the 1920s, my mother had two friends who became widows. These ladies seemed glamorous to me, always dressed in black and draped with soft silk scarves and veils. They were seductive and sexy, and I think they were regarded as such by men and women alike. To many women, though, they were also seen as a threat. In Victor Herbert's 1906 musical *The Red Mill*, there is a song that cautions: "A widow has ways, her experience pays. . . . It's this man tomorrow and that man today."

I can tell you, as a relative newcomer to widowhood, that such allure and intrigue are, at best, elusive. The reality for a widow of my age, that is to say, over seventy, is not the stuff of song. Even with some warning, such as a husband's longstanding illness, widowhood is a shock. I certainly was not prepared for it. My husband of nearly thirty years was Harrison Salisbury, author, journalist and *New York Times* editor. For much of his career, I accompanied him on the exotic trips he took to such places as Siberia, Mongolia, China and Tibet. I was sure we would die together, crashing down in a small airplane in some obscure country.

The jolt of his dying of heart failure while I was driving us home from a holiday weekend so stunned me that, though I thought I was acting normally, for months I simply existed. Idly, I'd go from room to room, unable to deal with anything more than just getting through each day. My family and friends stood by me, and eventually time and coping with my husband's papers and books brought me back. Today, many years later, in spite of the loneliness (or maybe because of it), I am leading a fuller social life.

But the social circuits to which I've tried to reconnect are not quite as welcoming to me as they once were. I'm not asking for a medal for getting through the first phase, which experts call the toughest, of my widowhood. But I somehow expected to have been treated with a bit more sensitivity than I've encountered. It would help if we widows could be thought of as people, not regarded as something left over, marginalized, extra.

Sometimes our desire to be viewed as whole individuals is hampered by what I believe is a double standard, stemming from perceptions about sex and age. A man who loses his wife, for example, almost immediately becomes desirable to women, especially hostesses planning dinner parties. A woman left alone can be neglected or forgotten, not purposely but because of social customs and prevailing attitudes. When I asked the director of an organization my husband belonged to and whose events we always attended together, "What do you do with people like me?" she replied, "We drop you." Occasionally, I run into people I used to see with my husband, and they act surprised ("Oh, are you here?"), as if I had died too and had just risen from my grave. It would be more considerate if they would simply say, "How nice to see you."

It would help if we widows could be thought of as people, not regarded as something left over, marginalized, extra.

Granted, an older widower's cachet on the social circuit may be greater than that of his female counterpart simply because, statistically, women outlive men by several years. But numbers should have nothing to do with civility; that would be like saying young women who live in cities where they outnumber bachelors in their age group are somehow less deserving of common courtesy. One man I know refers to older widows as vultures. This crack, and the idea that anyone would apply it to me, actually stopped me from writing a condolence note to a gentleman I know who'd lost his wife. Foolishly, I passed on what would have been a thoughtful gesture for fear that he might think I had some ulterior motive.

Many people think widows are out for anything they can get, especially other women's husbands. I don't know where that idea comes from. None of the widows I know is like that. They are the same people they've always been, now trying to come to terms with an irreplaceable loss. It's more than a little presumptuous of men—or the women who worry we might steal them—to think that our late husbands' shoes might so readily be filled.

When married women can stay those undercurrents of suspicion, they can be of tremendous support to their widowed contemporaries. They could include us in their parties and ask another guest or couple to pick us up so we don't have to arrive alone. In social settings, they might try to think of new topics of conversation so that the past is not brought up all the time. (And invitations don't have to include men. Women friends can ask us to join them at a movie, serve on a committee—make us feel included.)

Sadly, some opportunities for friendship can be lost amid all the assumptions about widows and their expectations. An attractive widow I know in my age group was taken out to dinner several times by a man who obviously enjoyed her company. One night he asked her if she'd ever considered getting married again, and she said no, it hadn't occurred to her. He never called her again. But why? Just because a woman doesn't wish to remarry doesn't mean she doesn't want companionship.

Maybe such misunderstandings could be avoided if widows of my age took a cue from women raised in the postfeminist era. Theoretically, at least, they're much more open in their dealings with members of the opposite sex. For them, the very act of, say, phoning a man is as common as stepping out without wearing gloves. But for women who entered their adulthood in the 1930s, as I did, it can take days, never mind hours, to work up the nerve to call a gentleman. I have discovered, though, to my great pleasure, that the results can be pleasantly surprising.

A while ago I was given two tickets to a birthday celebration for a prominent friend and felt it was suitable to have a male escort. Whom did I dare ask? Although I finally settled on a man whose family I'd known for many, many years, I was still nervous about issuing the invitation: How would I feel if he said he couldn't come? Would I believe him? Would I venture to ask anyone again? To my relief, he said he would be delighted to attend, and at the party it was clear that he enjoyed himself immensely. When the evening was over, I was happy that times, indeed, had changed.

As outmoded and impractical social conventions continue to slip away, relationships between men and women of all ages can become easier and more rewarding. That's good news for widows. After all, we are not asking for much: just to be seen as the women we are, with our own sensibilities and feelings. Lucky if love comes along, but happy to be asked out for ice cream.

VII
LIFE OF THE PARTY

Host or guest, everyone has a part to play.
What's yours?

Speak Easy

⸺. by Diana McLellan .⸺

It's a curious thing, isn't it, that some rather sophisticated people have trouble with small talk. That's a pity, because whether it's spread over a long dinner party, launched aboard a yacht or struck up on the fly with attractive strangers in a buffet line, great small talk does what it's always done: It wins new friends, lifts spirits into a celebratory mood and evokes the best in others. It amuses, delights and challenges. Most important these days, it clearly marks the great divide between the workaday, rush-rush-gotta-go world and a social occasion.

At least, that's how it works in theory. Where I live, in Washington, D.C., you simply can't escape political shoptalk. It's as much a part of the social scene as ice cubes—like entertainment in L.A., sports in Chicago and fashion in New York City. Traditionally, good small talk only springs from the airy queries that prompt personal flights of fancy: "Do you remember your first oyster?" "What makes you happiest in life?" "Tell me what you're reading." It recoils from status snooping. That said, I can report that one nosy friend has perfected a technique that elicits exactly what she yearns to know from even the sniffiest Eurosnob, without crossing the line: "You must be the head of a fabulously powerful diamond cartel," she coos, late in a dinner conversation. Or, at cocktails: "Let me guess—you're either the mistress of a king or an incredibly successful defense attorney."

"There's no harm in a little flattery in small talk," observes one of Washington's best small-talkers. She herself can conduct witty discourses on topics ranging from treasure-hunting to Welsh witchcraft. Although she avoids conversational heavy lifting—abortion, religion and, unless it's a strictly political event, politics—others are finding that, in the wake of '90s-style frivolity, issues of substance are acceptable grist for the small-talk mill.

Nonetheless, if you adhere to the 1860s etiquette-book caution against "argument on points likely to lead to the expression of strong feelings," there are plenty of other topics to smack your lips over: theater, film, books, life with cable or without television, exercise gadgetry, the latest island discovery or cutting-edge riffs from *The New York Times'* science pages. I remember one luncheon at which the lobster salad was washed down with lots of Champagne and an hour's witty debate on the pros and cons of the Nouveau Informality, exemplified by the White House sending out typewritten invitations to a ladies' tea.

If you're going to gossip, it's wise to arrive with something nice and fresh. One well-known raconteuse, when she runs short, races over to a large newsstand before a party, flips though both obscure intellectual monthlies and the trashiest tabloids and then turns up bursting with juice. In Washington, where gossip is practically currency, the real pros often utilize the "you call and I'll raise" ploy. They allow someone else to bring up the hot issue and then simply pile on the tastiest inside details they know. "That way," it was once explained to me, "you don't get the blabbermouth reputation—just the credit for knowing."

One thing not all Americans know is that in some parts of the globe, the question "What do you do?" is the conversational equivalent of guzzling from your finger bowl. I've met foreigners so shocked when quizzed about their work that they retaliate with creative responses: "I am chief anchovy-curler at the British embassy." "I put the little worm in our Mexican liquor bottles." "I am our president's taster."

In times past, knocking either the host's morals (of course, he's a saint!) or his cuisine (of course, it's perfect!) was a no-no. Today, it seems cruel to rob sincere foodies of the latter pleasure.

One thing not all Americans know is that in some parts of the globe, the question "What do you do?" is the conversational equivalent of guzzling from your finger bowl.

Besides, food can redirect the conversational traffic quite nicely. I was once delightfully regaled over the consommé by a dinner partner who had witnessed a well-known actor's glass eye falling into his soup; another, over oysters, quoted Oscar Wilde: "The world was my oyster, but I used the wrong fork." Someone once wrote that for every ten jokes, you make a hundred enemies, but James Boswell's 1784 rule that "No innocent species of wit or pleasantry should be suppressed" still applies. Arnaud de Borchgrave, the journalist and businessman, even insists that "Jokes are always good small talk, even at funerals." He usually stockpiles enough for a three-day yachting cruise—"But having to keep it up any longer than that is a nightmare."

And what of name-dropping? My 1860s *Etiquette for Gentlemen* damns it thoroughly: "Above all, never drag in the names of distinguished persons to whom you may be related or who may be numbered among your friends."

That's a bit much to ask more than a century later, a far naughtier time despite our attention to political correctness. But I've noticed that today's most successful name-droppers cloak their crowing in self-deprecation: "Hillary and I agree we're such awful klutzes in the kitchen that we're better off staying out." "I haven't had a chance to have the car washed because the queen was in town on a private visit." Much is made of how the president's helicopter ruins one's azaleas or what a nuisance it is to dine out with the Secret Service in tow.

Oscar Wilde rehearsed a lot of his small talk before leaving home—including, no doubt, his oyster-fork line. Extreme? Perhaps. But one live wire I know scribbles three delicious new topics inside a matchbook cover before an evening out and peeks to remind himself whenever the well runs dry. Another, a woman with a reputation for vast knowledge, often calls the chatty florist who handles some of the best parties in town to find out who'll be there and simply does her homework before she sallies forth.

On the embassy circuit, it's been my observation that most Frenchmen adore gossip, particularly about politicians; Latins are fond of literature or the arts; Argentineans, horses; Germans go for Big Issues; Britons, flirting or self-effacing wit. Prince Charles once kept a woman I know convulsed with the tale of his new electric toothbrush going berserk, covering himself and his royal bathroom with flying paste.

Of course, small talk with royalty can be tricky. Many otherwise worldly folk find themselves tongue-tied or burbling, wondering if they're really supposed to say things like "And how is Her Majesty the Queen?" (The answer is yes, but keep the rest simple: A noted statesman/philanthropist once spoke with the queen about "the necessity of elements of refurbishment" in the embassy; the arch phrase set off gales of giggles around the court for weeks.)

Patrick Daly, a veteran of the State Department's protocol office, knows all about squiring royal visitors around. "It's better to chat of figures in the arts or sports from the king or queen's country rather than politicians," he advises. "There are no universally beloved political leaders, unless you're speaking to that leader's sister or son." Forget that your new chum's land has the biggest cockroaches you've ever seen or no bathrooms. If you're together for a long time, ask how his countrymen handle matters that are of interest to you: sending children away to school, for instance, or dealing with aged parents.

For the nonroyal host or hostess, perhaps the best recipe for small talk came from poet and satirist Jonathan Swift (1667–1745), who compared conversation to carving a roast in a gentleman's house:

> *Give no more to every guest*
> *Than he's able to digest.*
> *Give him always of the prime,*
> *And but little at a time.*
> *And that you may have your due,*
> *Let your neighbor carve for you.*

Naturally, that was before the birth of sinfully expensive political fund-raising dinners. Yet even at those high-octane events, where Big Talk rules, the night gets its real sparkle the old-fashioned way—table by table, place card by place card, tit for tat—from good small talk.

Don't Forget the Punch Line

by David Brown

A man was sitting beside a well-dressed woman on an airplane. The woman was wearing a diamond ring so stunning that the man could not resist complimenting her on it.

"Oh, thank you," she said, "but unfortunately it comes with a curse . . . the Plotnick curse."

Puzzled, the man asked, "What's that?"

"Mr. Plotnick."

When the late comedian Myron Cohen told that story, it was enhanced by his sharp timing, deft inflections and signature deadpan expression. Enviable qualities, to be sure, for anybody aspiring to hold an audience of five or five thousand. Few of us could hope for the storytelling finesse of Cohen.

Not long ago, when conversation was king, men and women with the storyteller's gift were invited everywhere for their ability to crack up gatherings with hilarious jokes or tales of their own—or somebody else's—haplessness. We may not all have the knack for telling a good story, yet inevitably we find ourselves in social settings where the ability to do so comes in handy. One could argue, in fact, that practicing a little, or at least thinking about your technique, is a sign of respect for fellow guests, not to mention your host or hostess.

In the interest of good manners but mostly good fun, I will attempt to impart some of the secrets of good storytelling. My credentials for teaching you how to become the life, rather than the leper, of the party are reasonably sound: early years as a comedy writer for the radio, screen and stage star Eddie Cantor, and many additional years working in Hollywood and on Broadway, where storytelling is a finely honed art.

Listen and perhaps you will learn.

Just as a joke should have a punch line—the signal to laugh—your story should have a point. It should be about something: your aunt Minnie's favorite earrings, which had to be fished out of a subway grating, or your mistakenly boarding a plane to Minneapolis (instead of Denver) with an expired credit card. Whatever, as Bob Dole used to say, you must tell it in a loud, confident voice, milking the details, but also reading your audience carefully for any signs of listener fatigue (in which case you should step up the pace).

Depending on the nature of the story, you may want to embellish it a little; if the story needs more juice, you may want to embellish it a lot. You're not under oath. If you're hopeless at storytelling—sure to flub the punch line or bore your listeners with deadening delivery—encourage someone else to do the honors. "Harry," you might say, "tell us about the time you were mistaken for an ax murderer and Betty refused to identify you."

Making yourself the butt of a story works best. My two jungle stories are examples. I use them shamelessly. When my wife, the brilliant magazine editor Helen Gurley Brown, ventured to climb to the top of a peak in the Rarotonga rain forest, I, faint with exhaustion, opted to sit on a log halfway up to await her return. I crouched in terror as the sun went down and all manner of jungle beasts screeched around me. Finally, the snap of a twig sent me leaping in fright, which is how my wife and her group found me, huddled under a tree, eyes shut.

Similarly, I was coerced by my wife into the Amazon jungle near Manaus once again to risk cardiac arrest, this time from an encounter with a crocodile or piranha. We looked, listened and trod warily, but the only beasts we saw were at the hotel's small zoo.

You'll find you can make a so-so story scintillating by acquiring another trait of the successful raconteur: confidence. People in show business, of course, call it stage presence. You must believe in your power to hold the audience. Effective storytellers can make their listeners laugh at jokes they don't even get. Any wavering in your delivery will dilute the story and weaken your listeners' participation.

To get laughs at someone else's expense, meanwhile, it's best to be friends with your prey. But if you're a Jerry Seinfeld, you can also get away with it through sheer comedic genius. He once characterized Gary Shandling, the incandescent star of cable's sorely missed "The Larry Sanders Show," as so poor "he has only one Porsche." Seinfeld, who reportedly earned $225 million in 1998 alone, said, "I don't get out of bed for one Porsche. That's public transportation to me—the courtesy bus. Sometimes I just park and leave the damn thing."

Knowing your audience is just as important as knowing your victim. When Henny Youngman, the ruler of the one-liners, told a WASP crowd once that Jewish women won't make love with the lights on because they can't stand seeing their husbands enjoy themselves, only a few people laughed. Likewise, tales that depend on four-letter words or sexual innuendo should never be told in uncharted company. The response can be chilling. The same may be said for jokes lampooning or savaging a political figure—unless you know the politics of the group with whom you're socializing.

Truly off-color stories should only be heard by the right crowd. Comedian George Burns told the most offensive ones, but they were the funniest. The tradition survives at the Friars Club roasts, where there is no depth of vulgarity to which comedy cannot descend. Jackie Mason's stand-up routines take no prisoners and offend everyone, yet his audiences are usually too convulsed with laughter to take umbrage. But, again, it's all in the telling: Bob Hope and Red Buttons never used four-letter words or risqué stories, but they always managed to get the big laughs.

One more thing: Never begin with "I've got a great joke." TV personality Gene Shalit always responds by saying, "I'll be the judge of that." It's best to start more modestly. Don't rush it. The humor is in the details. Myron Cohen could spin out a funny story for a half-hour, festooning it with hilarious asides. And he was a genius with dialect; anyone who isn't should not attempt it.

To sum up, a good storyteller observes the following rules:

- Memorize the story, particularly the punch line if it's a joke.
- Be so confident in the telling that listeners will laugh even if the story isn't funny.
- Avoid dialect unless you're a master of it.
- Know your audience.
- Never say, "Here's the funniest story I've ever heard."
- Try—please try—to remember how often you have told the story.
- Timing is crucial. Leave space for the laugh—or, alas, the deafening silence.

Utterly Shameless

by Letitia Baldrige

The evening had been pleasant. My husband and I were contentedly chatting with friends during the cocktail hour at a formal dinner. The guest of honor was the new executive director of a large nonprofit organization, and our hosts were the chairman of the board of trustees and his wife. They'd invited one hundred people to the seated dinner (ten round tables of ten) in their beautiful home and had labored over an intelligent seating plan that would work to the new director's best advantage.

So I was particularly incredulous when I caught sight of a well-known pair of social climbers slipping behind the coromandel screens concealing the dining area to inspect the seating arrangements. Obviously disappointed in where they'd been placed, the nefarious duo set about changing the place cards in order to seat themselves beside the most prominent and glamorous people in attendance. After leading their guests into dinner, the hosts discovered, as they later described it to me, that they'd been "sabotaged."

To say that the place-card changers' conduct was rude is an understatement. A rude person is often careless and unthinking but is usually too fast-moving to realize just how much he or she has offended others. Shameless people, on the other hand, often know full well when they're doing something mean-spirited or overly self-serving. Like those of the place-card changers, their actions are more calculated. It doesn't bother them to be thought of as nasty.

Shamelessness is variously defined as indecent, audacious, brazen or impudent behavior. One thing's certain: You almost always know it when you see it, and we're seeing plenty of it these days. We're nearly immune to it in professional sports, where athletes now berate, punch, slash, kick and spit at other athletes and even bystanders with impunity. Shame, all too often, brings fame. An obscure member of Congress can derail an opponent's bill and elbow his way into the headlines with a sensational attack worthy of the trash-TV shows (repositories of the worst displays of shamelessness to be found anywhere). The fact that such unsavory behavior might be rewarded as readily as it might be condemned—aren't we the nation that reveres "shock jocks" more than statesmen?—only encourages it. If there's more of this consequences-be-damned behavior today, it may also have something to do with the uprootedness of our lives: Some people couldn't care less about how their actions affect others, reasoning with a shrug, "I'll never see them again, anyway."

Absolved, in their own minds, at least, of all responsibility, the shameless go shopping. First stop: the china store, where fine crystal and silver are purchased for a dinner party, only to be returned afterward with the explanation that "they didn't really work with the color scheme of our dining room." (Stores especially object when the customer hasn't even bothered to thoroughly wash the new plates!) Next stop: the designer boutique at a favorite department store, where a dress is purchased from the latest collection. It's worn to a huge fundraiser, then returned for credit a couple of days later with the excuse: "It really doesn't fit at all." (A salesperson once said with resignation, "I always know what was served at dinner, because there's inevitably a spot of consommé or chocolate sauce somewhere on the garment.")

Historically, stores have looked the other way, but some are beginning to take a harder line on abuses of return policies. That's probably a very good thing. It doesn't seem fair to let the shameless off the hook. To do so is to make the rest of us a party to their crassness. Perhaps I should have said something to the place-card bandits, since I was the one who caught them in the act. Obviously, I would not have wanted to embarrass my hosts with a scene. But maybe mentioning something quietly or even just letting the culprits know they were being watched—with, ahem, the right-sounding cough—might have been enough to deter them.

Consider another social situation in which propriety, never mind decency, seems to dictate that there be a response: You're enjoying the cocktail conversation when someone in your pod utters an ethnic or racial slur. Such words hit you with the force of a sharp blow. You can always stand there wishing for the proverbial hole in the floor to open and swallow you up; or you can ameliorate the situation by expressing your discomfort and offense. Bear in mind that saying something at moments like these takes not only courage but plenty of tact. And there can be repercussions: I'm told of a man who confronted a bigoted party guest only to find himself and his wife frozen out of the social circuit in their new town. The good news is that they're probably a couple who sleep pretty well at night.

Alas, the social circuit does seem to provide a perfect breeding ground for acts of shamelessness; unfortunately, we can't find some nice, neat solution to every one of them. How best, for example, to deal with those who suddenly deem it convenient to "find religion," because joining a particular church or synagogue will give them entrée to important business contacts? Or people who lie about how much they've donated to charity? Or those who claim they attended Harvard, Yale or Princeton when they didn't? Or women who brag about their "real" jewelry when it's fake, or men who boast about illustrious ancestors they never had?

The desire to get even with the perpetrator of a shameless act is only human. The story comes to mind of a man who, while checking his luggage at the airport, loudly berated the skycap over some small transgression. The porter took this abuse in silence while others sympathetically looked on.

"Why didn't you say something?" one of them asked later.

"Didn't have to. The man is going to Chicago," the skycap said calmly, "but his luggage is going to L.A."

Revenge may be sweet, but it's never going to remove the evil cloud of shamelessness from the land. And while calling the callous on their misdeeds may at times be appropriate, its lasting impact is questionable. (How do you reach people who are too self-involved to hear you, anyway?) The best hope for eliminating the stony indifference of shamelessness may be to teach—and reteach—our children, grandchildren and other young people the value of respect for others. To miss a golden opportunity to plant such a good seed in a child's mind, well, that would be a real shame.

Jetiquette

———• by Lyle Crowley •———

With a nod to the captain, I stepped aboard the Cessna Citation V, its engines humming, and followed my host, a top fashion designer, to the rear of the cabin. Sliding into a choice forward-facing seat, admiring the smooth, tanned leather, I eyed the bountiful fruit-and-cheese platters along the walls. All was bliss until I caught the glare of a grim-faced executive, the last to board, now perched on a backless seat that doubled, as is the way with smaller jets, as the commode. By the time I feebly offered to switch seats he waved me back with no small amount of sarcasm. "That's okay," he said. "So long as you're comfortable." We hadn't even left the ground, and already I was an outcast.

Well, almost. If you've made it onboard, you've made it: No society ball, no four-star dinner, no invitation to a country house can match the cachet of soaring above it all on some form of private aircraft. Small wonder Jacqueline Onassis once observed, "People will sell their souls for a free ride on an airplane." Yes, this rarefied pleasure does have its price—for guest and host. In committing my aforementioned sin, I'd temporarily lost sight of this fact. What may appear to be a casual atmosphere is, in fact, laden with protocol, a subtle collection of civilities you might call *jetiquette*.

If you've been invited to fly down to Lord Loftable's private resort, your foremost responsibility is to arrive at the airport on time. The plane will be drinking up fuel at a rate you don't want to know about. Latecomers who offer to chip in for the wasted gas will only further confirm their lack of breeding. Understand that the same rule does not apply to your host. As one pilot puts it: "That's the whole reason he bought the plane—so *he* can be late. That relieves so much of the stress of traveling."

Guests have other duties to consider before flight time. Minimalist packing is the rule. (Few private-jet owners crisscross the globe in the spaciousness of the 737 Doris Duke owned.) Bringing golf clubs and skis is acceptable, but you should inquire ahead of time about the plane's size. Your host will be impressed with your knowledge of varying load capacities. As for the gifts you'll pick up during those frequent refueling stops that small planes require, ship them home. (Exceptions might be made for cashmere sweaters from Shannon.) Spare yourself the chagrin of the executive who bought boxes of talking toy birds for his children, only to have them chirp and caw uncontrollably after a bit of turbulence. Since real birds cannot be sent by Federal Express, a bullion trader once jetted to his private island along with twenty-five flamingos—wrapped up, their legs folded, and honking with understandable displeasure.

There may be no way of knowing whether you'll be flying with fowl, but the very look of a plane can tell you much about your host. Designer Rose Tarlow, who revamped a Gulfstream for a client, says the interior should be "so simple that it's barely noticeable." Excess has no place. "Just use beautiful fabrics and leathers." (Owners: Avoid the tragedy that became the laughingstock of an exclusive Teterboro, New Jersey, hangar. The small white stars misguidedly painted across its top resembled heaps of bird droppings.)

Entertainment can make or break a trip. Having amusements

on hand for children—crayons, coloring books, playing cards—is essential: Kids must be kept occupied for reasons obvious to anyone who's ever flown with them. Thoughtful hosts usually see to this, as well as to adult fare. One company executive always treats his guests to the "Civil War" video series. (Seen it? You'll just have to grin and bear it.) Other offerings include personal CD players, for more than just guest use: Riding in the helicopter of a well-known financier, I turned to ask him a question but got no reply; he was wired into a Discam. Such haughtiness may have violated the spirit of jetiquette, but then again, he was providing me with the most coveted route back to Manhattan from the Hamptons.

> Once in the air, there's nothing wrong with showing your fear when the going gets rough; however, the host is never expected to apologize for a bumpy ride.

After takeoff—"a true flier would call it 'wheels up,'" says one guest fluent in the language of private flight—fruit, smoked salmon, sandwiches and various breads might be served. Maybe you'll receive a taste of the legendary lavishness of Hugh Hefner's plane, but be grateful for cheese and crackers. Mindful hosts have someone check beforehand to see if guests have special dietary needs.

Such details often fall to the pilot, who can play the stoic airborne equivalent of Mr. Stevens in *The Remains of the Day*. A discreet pilot would know, for instance, never to load the cabin's CD player with the soundtrack of your mistress' latest show—particularly on family outings. "Flying the airplane becomes the easiest part," says a Citation V pilot for . . . well, he's not telling.

But the pilot-employer relationship can be tested. Hosts have been known to demand that planes be flown despite foreboding weather fronts. In the Rockies, it's called The Last Plane Out of Aspen, a game that ranks with chicken in the annals of machismo. In such cases, passengers may ask to be released from the plane without explanation—while they're still on the tarmac, that is. Once in the air, there's nothing wrong with showing your fear when the going gets rough; however, the host is never expected to apologize for a bumpy ride. In fact, nothing will show your breeding better than lifting your green, patrician chin and cheerfully thanking the pilot for doing a good job under difficult circumstances.

Veterans of the private skies know that no one should ever be tipped after a flight. And don't even dream of asking your host if you can help cover costs. Do, however, thank the crew (it will be remembered) and consider sending a small gift to your host—something for the plane, such as a sleeping mask.

Certain people, of course, are naturals at the nuances of jetiquette. But what's the official line? "Travel light," says etiquette expert Nancy Tuckerman. "And keep quiet, even in a storm. Unless, of course, you see another plane headed your way."

Manners, too, have their exceptions.

Long Live the Gracious Host

by Nancy Tuckerman

he days when Newport, Rhode Island, was the scene of elegant house parties for which guests arrived by private railroad car—ladies' maids and trunks filled with clothes in tow—are rife with material for a contemporary screenwriter's imagination. The modern reality of the host/houseguest relationship is, of course, a radically different affair. On the surface, that is. As the coauthor of *The Amy Vanderbilt Complete Book of Etiquette*, I've discovered that after peeling away all the pretense and opulence of ages past, the basics of good manners haven't really changed much. In a curious way, what was expected of gracious hosts in old Newport is not, in principle, so different from what one might reasonably expect of them today.

Some people are born hosts, blessed with a certain finesse, an aptitude for entertaining. They know just how to make their guests feel as if they'd never left home. And what's remarkable is that when faced with some catastrophe, such as a tornado whipping through the area and taking with it their water and electricity, they simply smile, unfazed, and manage to keep things under control. A confident, relaxed host is decidedly someone to admire and emulate: She's the one who's always well organized, does what's sensible, uses her intuition and doesn't fall apart like a paper napkin if it pours rain in the middle of her picnic.

My turn as a weekend host began some fifteen years ago, when

I rented a house in the foothills of the Berkshires. Just as you never fully understand the rules (and rule breakers) of the road until you get behind the wheel yourself, I could finally appreciate all that it took to keep my guests happy—and keep my wits in the process. I found that even the most well bred among us are capable of missteps when it comes to sleeping under a friend's roof. But rather than bemoan the foibles of my well-meaning guests (well, most of them were well meaning), I thought about what I might do in my role as host to make this social compact more satisfying to both sides. It wasn't always easy, mind you: Have you ever tried putting on a brave front when your company shows up with an unexpected companion—their dog?

> There was a lot more to ensuring a good time for all than taking care not to invite a Montague and a Capulet on the same weekend.

Still, as the seasons passed outside my mountain retreat I came to learn some of the secrets of the hosts I'd most admired over the years. There was a lot more to ensuring a good time for all than taking care not to invite a Montague and a Capulet on the same weekend. So much for the more obvious; it's the more practical we sometimes overlook in the houseguest gambit.

Experienced hosts know, for example, to extend their invitations weeks ahead of time, especially those for holiday weekends. That not only helps guarantee that your would-be guests will be available, it also means they're less likely to imagine they're your second choice. And when plans are being firmed up, it's important to be specific as to when guests should arrive and, equally important, leave. I learned the particular usefulness of this "small" point one endless Sunday. I had assumed my guests would be departing after lunch. Not so. As the long afternoon turned into the cocktail hour, I found I had an unplanned meal on my hands—and an empty fridge. Luckily, the local inn was open, but the price I paid for my assumption was the bill for four dinners.

Generally speaking, before you invite friends for the weekend it's a good idea to make a list of helpful things to tell them. Otherwise you might forget, say, to remind a man that he'll need his dinner jacket or let a woman know that you'll be going to a club where slacks are not allowed in the dining room after six.

To carry the bonhomie of anticipation into your guests' stay itself, providing them with a comfortable bedroom—and especially a comfortable bed—is crucial. Perhaps that seems understood, yet I once spent the night in a perfectly equipped guest room with a magnificent antique canopy bed, the mattress of which had to have been stuffed with the original horsehair. As I attempted to sleep on this lumpy and uneven relic, it became clear that my host (I believe I was referring to her by another term at that moment) had never spent a night in this room.

The only way to test a bed and, indeed, assess the overall acceptability of a guest room is to spend a night in it yourself. Once you do, you'll have a much greater appreciation of hosts who provide good lighting for reading in bed, adequate drawer and closet space, extra pillows and blankets, and opaque window shades. The ideal guest room might also contain a luggage rack, paper and pens, a folding umbrella, local sightseeing brochures, recent magazines and carefully chosen books. Not to be overlooked are those seemingly incidental touches, such as proper skirt and trouser hangers—not wire ones from the dry cleaner—and fresh soaps for the bathroom basin and bathtub.

As important as creature comforts can be, seeing to the trickier matter of filling your guests' waking hours can be where a host's true aplomb comes into play. Naturally, much depends on the tastes and interests of your company. Many friends who visit me like nothing better than to be let loose on the Appalachian trail for an all-day hike. (The only social engagement they want is with the deer!) Then there are those who prefer getting their exercise on a country-club dance floor. Either way, guests should always be encouraged to make their wishes known. That frees you up to state your own need for some time alone during the weekend, whether it's to take care of household chores or to simply put your feet up so you can catch your breath. Such candor works to everyone's advantage, since guests like to feel they can go off on their own for antiquing, playing a round of golf or whatever. Along these lines, if you're in the habit of attending religious services, let your guests know in advance and offer them the option of joining you.

It's never rude, in fact, to be direct about any of your rituals, not to mention your idiosyncrasies. Go ahead and ask your guests to conserve hot water or take off their boots before coming into the house. It is your home after all, and even habits that might seem trivial to others should be respected. Rather than intimidating your callers, this sort of openness can make them feel more at ease. Relaxed guests who understand what's expected of them surely beat nervous, jumpy ones who worry at every turn about committing a faux pas.

But hosts can't expect their overnight guests to be perfect, or, in the directive of a 1924 etiquette book I have, "never disagreeable, never quarrelsome, never grouchy." In fact, most hosts have a list of pet peeves. The one I hear most frequently is that guests don't check their room and bath before leaving. (It's a bore to have to mail back forgotten articles.) The list also includes guests who insist upon going along on grocery-shopping trips, even if they've been asked not to. And there is one annoyance at the top of my own list: guests who smoke without having asked for permission.

Technology's double-edged sword has given us the visitor who thoughtlessly uses a cellular phone in the company of others. But guests are not the only high-tech offenders. I still cringe when I recall the couple who, after changing their mind about having invited another couple for the weekend, sent their friends a fax saying their children had come down with chickenpox. There is a certain justice in the fact that their would-be lodgers were already en route, so the chagrined hosts were forced to spend the entire weekend painfully aware of the *mensonge pieux* awaiting their guests back home.

High-tech or low, the guests who most impress me are the ones who volunteer to bring some kind of food for a weekend meal: a casserole or fresh pasta. And what about a wicker basket filled with fruit or jams? Or even a thoughtful assortment of rented videos? But the best present of all—one that comes after my company has left—is an appreciative thank-you letter, written with warmth and sincerity. The guests who remember that gesture are the ones I want to invite back.

Please Don't Interrupt

• by Barbara Howar •

I was interrupting before it was trendy. It was a handy survival skill for a nice southern debutante thrust into political Washington in the days when women only got a word in edgewise when the men paused for breath. Believe me, barging into those windy monologues was an audacious alternative in a time and a town where young ladies too often heard risked being seldom seen. Now, of course, everybody interrupts. Constantly.

Interrupting has become such a tiresome fact of life that it's arguably the most spontaneous intercourse between the sexes today. Men and women all across the country verbally wrestle each other to the mat in clubs and pubs, dining rooms and boardrooms, each exercising an inalienable right to rudeness. We could blame all this on the powerful influence of television, and we would be partly right. On TV, good and bad behavior is not only reflected but learned. Grabbing the vocal spotlight and shouting the final word has become a matter of every man (or woman) for himself. Television awards no points for good deportment.

But it's too easy to blame television alone for the interrupt-athon that now passes for conversation. The tube does help legit-imize the national boorishness by constantly exposing viewers to politicians and pop know-it-alls cutting each other off at the oral pass. Witnessing this daily spectacle can numb us into thinking that—as in the case of poor grammar so often used it seems the norm—interrupting is acceptable; that it's just another modern nuisance like the beeper and call waiting and cell phones and unso-licited fax messages.

The culprit, alas, isn't a household appliance; it's we and our immediate peers—everyone with whom we now hotly cross talk in what were once congenial lunchtime or after-dinner discussions. Even the more cultivated of my friends and acquaintances, having long since elevated spirited dissension to an art form, are subject to interrupting their interrupters.

Time was, and not so long ago, people argued just as much but with civility and subtlety. It's a combination that was often urged on me by the late and legendary Washington wit Alice Roosevelt Longworth, who insisted the secret to winning any debate was genteel restraint. "It's not only a sign of breeding to let your opponent have his turn," she advised with a sly smile, "but it adds deliciously to the shock value of a wicked retort."

It does something else just as important: It allows time for the considered response. That very notion is about as quaint as it is radical in a world of instant opinions. What's become of the exchange dynamic of conversation? It seems to have been replaced by a layering dynamic. The more parties to the conversation, the more layers, forming a verbal Vesuvius.

Maybe what we're seeing—rather, hearing—are the results of a culture in which we're all too fascinated with the sound of our own voices. Anybody else's voice becomes intrusive, so much filler to be endured until, time's up, it's my turn again. Your lips may still be moving, but if I am ready to speak, well, here goes. The once embarrassing non sequitur is a mainstay of these brave new verbal gymnastics.

Certainly the clock is the enemy of illuminating conversation, the ticking force behind our manic overlapping. A case of so much to say, so little time. Plus a democratic determination to put forth our two cents' worth. "It's a peculiarly American thing, this passion to intrude," observed a visiting British friend. And if the practice of butting in has upped the national volume, it's because both sexes are increasingly guilty of the intrusion. Even in my native South, where tradition dies hard, the deferential pause has fallen victim to *quietus interruptus* in parlors once filled by demurring, deferring ladies.

> What's become of the exchange dynamic of conversation? It seems to have been replaced by a layering dynamic.

No one would want to return to the days when women in mixed company who wanted to comment on anything weightier than skirt lengths had to shout to be heard. Still, as author and Washington hostess Sally Quinn says, "I guess we're all pretty much equal-opportunity interrupters these days."

Manners minding, though, isn't a matter of gender. And if there's no way we're going to quit interrupting one another altogether—and there isn't—there's nothing to keep us from injecting a bit of decorum into the exercise. What's to stop any of us, for example, from uttering a simple "Excuse me" if we've spoken before our turn? Pardon begging is also permissible before chiming in to dispute or agree with somebody's stated premise. And difficult though it may be, we should attempt, at least, to hold our tongues when the speaker is elderly and not fully accustomed to the breakneck pace at which many of us—particularly those in communications—communicate with one another today. (Never, come hell or high water, should we interrupt a stutterer.)

All of that said, there are times—rare, mind you—when interrupting can be a sign of social savvy. In truth, a by-your-leave even from those supplying the thought we've momentarily lost could couth things up considerably. Or what about graciously helping extricate a foot from a mouth—or a foot on its way there. (What I wouldn't give to have been saved by a well-timed bit of *interruptus* on more occasions than I care to remember.)

Sure, it would be a lot more civilized if, in the future, we could all simply take a number, just like at the fish market, and speak only when our turn comes up. Dream on. The glut of fact and rumor ahead are bound to keep us noisily vying to get in an edgewise word. And consider that the rules for cyber engagement have yet to be drafted. But guidelines for pursing loose lips, in the living room or the chat room, should, like all good manners, be built around respect. When everyone speaks at once, you don't get information, you get noise.

These are not preachings that I faithfully practice. Just how incapable of yielding the floor I can be recently hit me during a routine gabfest on an all-news cable station. Beamed in via satellite from L.A., I was linked to the New Jersey mother ship only by audio. Unable to make eye contact with the host or the garrulous guests beamed in from sundry other sites, I blindly lobbed my opinions to the camera. To wrest the airwaves back from unseen colleagues who usurped mine, I simply kicked up the decibel level and kept yakking into the microphone. Naturally, the others did likewise, creating a cacophony that made it impossible to understand anything that anyone was saying.

Which wasn't all bad.

VIII
THEY ALSO SERVE

*They ring up our groceries and
bring up our children. Yet sometimes we scarcely
know they exist. Our loss.*

Give Me the Civil Life

· by Anne Taylor Fleming ·

he other day in the market I was standing in the checkout line behind an attractive woman—blond, thin, well dressed. She had apparently left her check-cashing card at home and was berating the young woman behind the cash register for not accepting her check anyway.

"I know I don't have my ID," she snapped, pawing through her name-brand purse just the same. "But I've been coming here for years."

"I'm sorry, ma'am," the young woman said, "I'll have to call my boss. I've been told not to . . ."

"Well, then do it. I don't have forever, you know."

On my top-ten list of How You Know Civilization Is in Decline, this sort of behavior is number one. I see it often these days—on a street corner, in an elegant home, at a shop. I see women do it, I see men do it and I see kids do it, too: be rude and high-handed toward someone in a service position, someone economically beholden, someone unable to fight back.

Unkindness of any sort offends me deeply; unkindness from someone in control toward someone in a subordinate position, like the incident in the market, is the unkindest cut of all. It's so graceless, so demeaning, so . . . déclassé.

Early in my suburban '50s childhood, I was taught that "class" was of the essence, and one of the surest measures of it was not how you related upward, to the boss or the bank owner or the head of the garden club next door (that was the easy stuff), but how you related downward, to the clerks and cleaners, the valets and waitresses. It wasn't about money or the right schools; it was an attitude, how you carried yourself in the world and the ease with which you dealt with people—all manner of people. Those who exuded this hybrid of kindness never evidenced any brittle imperiousness toward those who attended them but instead displayed an assured grace. They were neither overbearing nor patronizing.

My mother always handled herself with a sort of easy warmth toward any and all who waited on her or who came into our house to perform various tasks, including looking after my sister and me or helping with dinner parties. I remember watching her bustle about before those parties, talking to the bartender or the canapé passer, her hair still in curlers, her makeup in place—so young, so pretty, so at home in her home. Without apology or condescension she managed, to my prepubescent ears, to hit a perfect note, one that said to the assembled staff: I respect you and your work.

I have never felt quite that same ease, the same clarity, in part because times have changed. Most of us don't run our houses with the attentiveness of our mothers. Many of us are juggling careers and families, husbands and households, and the stress fractures show, sometimes in a kind of overzealous managerial style. I have been the unhappy witness to angry scenes between women I like and the women they employ: a sharp-tongued dressing-down of an assistant, a tirade aimed at a tardy baby-sitter. Some of the shortouts are due to sheer overload, some to the complicated new hands women are playing.

I certainly don't mean to completely exempt men from this

indictment. Given the prefeminist "Father Knows Best" household of my childhood, I am just more habituated to the sometimes imperious ways of many men—their jocularity and assertiveness. How well I recall squirming through dinners at which dads would demand this or that of a waitress or a housekeeper, sometimes with stone-cold detachment. These men didn't think they were being rude or arrogant, but the inference was clear: We are of a different ilk, we are here solely to be served; you are here to serve us. This attitude has not vanished. I have seen it more recently manifested by posturing young men pumped up by brandy and bravado, well-dressed fellows too busy for thank-yous when their drinks are set before them in handsome barrooms.

> Are we turning into a nation of bullies for whom the social graces have all but been lost, specifically the grace of dealing with subordinates?

Are we turning into a nation of bullies for whom the social graces have all but been lost, specifically the grace of dealing with subordinates—the grace of all graces in my book, the thing that tells the most about us and the depth of our decency? What, after all, says more about the essence of our conduct, our very nature, than the way we treat people over whom we have some power?

Graciousness toward those who work for us can produce far more tangible benefits than just the satisfaction of doing the right thing. Not long ago, I had occasion to venture forth from my writer's cloister at home into a television newsroom on an extended assignment. I made it a point to talk to, be solicitous of—all right, seduce a little—those whose services I depended upon: drivers, hairdressers, makeup artists and stagehands. All reciprocated in kind, making me look and sound good—and, not incidentally, feel good.

There have been other times when I've been reminded of some basic human impulse to help—dare I say, serve—one another. When we in Los Angeles were digging out after the big earthquake in January 1994, there emerged a wonderful, if fleeting, sense of community—something rare in L.A., and in America, where the economic divisions between the haves and the have-nots are ever-widening, the tensions ever-escalating. For a postquake minute, those divisions disappeared. The freeways were down and the buses weren't running. As a result, some people were finding themselves in never-before-seen parts of town as they attempted to get to work themselves or take home from work a maid who'd perhaps been in their service for many years. There was an unusually high degree of civility and concern going back and forth; not phony concern, just a deep-down understanding of our shared plight, our shared humanity.

As I get older, I realize that the people I've admired most have been those who move between and among worlds—from the White House to their own houses—without a variance of behavior toward others, without a deviation in kindness or respect. That's class. That's what I would want said about myself, above all else.

A View from the Fridge

by Anthony Bourdain

I am a chef. Though I can be a terror in my kitchen, in the dining room of other restaurants I'm a pussycat. I am scrupulously polite and effusive in my praise. And I always tip 20 percent—at least. I'm also, I am told, not the most attentive of dinner companions. I can't help but be attuned, almost painfully at times, to every nuance around me. There are a number of things—simple, avoidable things—that can throw off the rhythms of even the best-run places. (I chronicled many of these missteps in my book *Kitchen Confidential*.) What have all my hours of standing before a stove taught me about sitting at a table?

Come on. Have a seat. Join me for dinner.

If the people at the table beside mine summon a busboy (the first available person in uniform), unable to distinguish him from their waiter, I cringe. I can tell you with near certainty that additional communication will now be required: The busboy—a member of a profession largely comprising newcomers to America's shores—will have to take aside the already harried waiter.

I also feel the waiter's pain when, without warning, a patron seated with friends at a table for four (a four-top) suddenly bolts to the bar for a cigarette. This often seems to occur just when the entrées for that table are about to be served or, as waiters say, are "in the window, ready for pickup." I know the electric shock that travels through the restaurant's spine and into the brainstem of the kitchen: The chef has that table's food up! It's sitting perilously under the destructive warmth of the heat lamps. Other orders are coming up around it, new ones are coming in, and the chef is beginning to freak; his lovely food is dying in front of him. It's a tiny, inconsequential move for the customer—a cigarette at the bar—but for the kitchen, particularly in a good restaurant, it can cause mad panic and much misery.

You want to see real suffering? Look at the face of a beleaguered maître d' with an unseated eight-top in the middle of a very busy dining room at 8:30 on a Saturday night. He's already cleared a huge block of valuable time in the reservation book, probably turned away two four-tops (who generally spend more money than one eight-top) from a seven o'clock seating. He's also kissed off any hope of turning the tables at 9:00 or even 10:00, for that matter. The party of eight yet to arrive represents a major leap of faith for him, an investment of not only the house's but the waiters' and busboys' money. Such no-shows are sticking it to the entire staff. (Along these lines, clowns who book at three or four restaurants on a given night and then neglect to cancel in a timely way are the blood enemies of restaurateurs and their staffs.)

Now, you might find this a bit disingenuous if you're thinking back to the night you arrived promptly and the restaurant wasn't able to seat you for fifteen minutes. Certainly, apologies—profuse ones—are in order. But all I can tell you is that it's in the restaurant's best interests to seat you as soon as possible. No one on my side of the table creates such delays; after all, it's bad for business when drop-ins see an overcrowded bar. Maybe I'm asking too much, but think about the imprecise science of seating the next time you're lingering over your coffee and nobody seems inclined to give you the bum's rush.

It's particularly loathsome when a customer who is displeased with his entrée vents his unhappiness on his waiter, as if willfully betrayed by his server. The simple distinction that his waiter did not cook his food is lost. Problem with the food? Ask nicely to have it replaced. Most times, you'll be surprised at how quickly and eagerly everyone responds. If the house has made a mistake, it's never a good idea to take it personally. No, nothing untoward is likely to happen to your entrée when it returns to the kitchen: It's your return to the restaurant that might be of concern. Customers who behave spitefully, angrily, simply flag themselves as rubes, even if they're wearing $2,000 suits. The whole restaurant will heave a sigh of relief at their exit, and on their next visit they will be relegated to the newest and possibly most inept waiter. The veterans won't want any part of them.

If the meal was good, should one send compliments to the chef? Yes!

Polite complaints or criticisms? By all means. They will be recorded, probably in the manager's log, or at the very least conveyed at the appropriate moment to the chef, who will, especially if he's heard the same comments before, do something in response. If the meal was good, should one send compliments to the chef? Yes! Believe it or not, the message will almost always be conveyed to the kitchen. We like it when our labors are appreciated. We remember it. And should we see you in our dining room again, we'll have a better picture of what you like and we'll be able to tip you off to what's new or special. We'll more than likely send *amuse-gueules* your way. I'm always happy to hear from the floor staff: "Table six are regular customers, man. Really good people. Can you send them something? What should they have?"

Sitting at my table, watching the action around me, I snicker at the miserable deuce a few tables away. They've been bullying their waiter mercilessly, and I can already see that he's conspiring with the busboy to clear their table as soon as the last forkful disappears into their maws. Later, over drinks with the waiters from the restaurant across the street, the terrible two-top will be discussed. Named. In the extended, inbred family of restaurant workers, the duo has been identified, their faces carved into the consciousness of a growing number of servers as irrevocably as the mugs gracing those wanted posters at the post office.

We all like places where they know our names and are familiar with our likes and dislikes. And, as in any complex relationship, one can, with just a few smiles and nods or the occasionally muttered thank-you, become special: a genuinely appreciated patron, a customer in good standing, a friend of the house. To demand special treatment is counterproductive. You simply banish yourself to the ranks of the undesirable herd. Most servers and chefs are grateful when given a measure of trust, and they would feel lessened if they betrayed it. The favorite customer at all restaurants is someone who by word or demeanor says, "I know you. I trust you. Give me your best shot." My decades in the business tell me we usually will.

For those few, those happy few, every extra effort is made. They are welcomed as warmly as, if not more warmly than, fellow employees, advised frankly and honestly on the best menu selections, and in every way treated like the home team instead of the visitors: "Great to see you. . . . Let me send you dessert? . . . A nice snifter of Calvados? . . . Thanks, and please come again."

Some Holiday Tips

by Francine Maroukian

No matter how early I start my Christmas countdown each year, there's never enough time. Santa may be coming to your town, but he seems to be invading mine. I feel put-upon, rushed and very busy. I start out with the best of intentions, vowing to be perfectly prepared and profoundly organized. But it's just so overwhelming. Some days the only contribution to holiday planning I can make is to look at magazine photos of people gold-leafing grapes—right before I fall asleep.

I try to keep myself on track by making lists. Big, beautiful, elaborate lists: Christmas-card lists, gift and grocery lists, and that grande dame, the gratuity list. The tradition of holiday tipping presents us with an opportunity to balance the books by proving we can give as good as we get. It is not a time to be thrifty. It is the time to reward that roster of people whose labor maintains the style to which we've become accustomed. And the grander the style, the longer the list.

There is nothing as revealing—and almost nothing as humbling—as sitting down with a blank piece of paper and writing the names of every person whose labor contributes to the quality of your life. Handymen, housekeepers, dog-walkers, eyebrow waxers, aromatherapists: Never have so many done so much. But don't assume they're willing to do it for so little. As a private caterer (with twenty years of experience), let me assure you that people in the service industry consider holiday tips "the big perk" of their jobs. They have their own version of seasonal gratuity lists and their own way of determining who's been naughty or nice. If that seems nervously near blackmail, ponder the situation from a more Zen-like chicken-and-egg perspective. Better service means bigger tips; bigger tips mean better service.

I would encourage you to make use of the political adage "Think globally/Act locally." Start your holiday tipping with the people closest to home. For city dwellers whose primary residence is a fully staffed building, this means porters (tips between $35 and $50), doormen (the $75 to $100 range) and the building's superintendent (whose gratuity is always larger than those of the doormen). Parking-garage attendants customarily receive tips of $50 to $100 (depending on your tipping pattern throughout the year). These cash tips, accompanied by a handwritten note, should be presented in person when schedules allow. It is appropriate (and appreciated) to do this early in the season, enabling recipients to use gratuities to enhance their own holiday gift giving.

> The tradition of holiday tipping presents us with an opportunity to balance the books by proving we can give as good as we get.

When many people hold the same position (as with doormen and most other urban service jobs), sometimes one of them stands out from the pack, always going that extra mile. You should feel free to tip him accordingly. A gentleman probably won't discuss that tip with his colleagues, but should word leak out, perhaps the others will take the hint.

For those who live in more countrified settings, acting locally means tipping anyone who works in your home on a regular basis (without being a full-time employee). A good rule of thumb is to match the gratuity's dollar amount with the cost of the service provided. A once-a-week pool person, for example, would receive his usual day rate as a tip; workers who come by twice a week should be rewarded with their weekly rates, and so on. (This applies in the town and the country: An appropriate tip for your weekly housecleaner in the city would be the equivalent of her weekly pay.)

No matter where you live, include those who make regular trips to your home, such as newspaper and dry-cleaning delivery people. (Tips for such individuals might be in the $20 to $40 range.)

After you act locally, think globally and consider the world of people who've become fixtures in your life by tending to your personal services. For the flawlessly groomed, who spend more time with their hairdressers than their husbands, there's no telling how extravagant seasonal gratuities can be. Through their manicured hands pass mountains of cash and miles of cashmere. One stylist, an avid equestrian known for giving good highlights, even corralled a hand-tooled saddle from a loyal client. But if you spend $250 or less per salon visit (cut and color), a good tipping schedule for support staff (like the shampoo person) is about $20, while stylists and colorists receive gratuities of $50 to $75.

For the others who keep you (and your pets) in perfect shape, tips range from $25 for manicurists (and similar aestheticians) to $50 for your masseuse and pet helpers. Personal trainers usually receive a dollar amount somewhere between the cost of one and two training sessions. Whatever the size or nature of the business, don't forget to tip the receptionists. They are the air-traffic controllers of the personal-service industry, able to bring you in for an immediate landing or leave you helplessly hovering, waiting for the first opening.

When services are more personal, cash tips are frequently accompanied by small gifts like boutique chocolates, a nice bottle of wine or Champagne (if you know the person drinks) or a fashionable accessory. In some cases—and often when real friendships have formed—cash is replaced altogether by a more significant gift.

In all my years as a caterer, I have never received cash over the holidays from my closest clients. But I have received very thoughtful gifts, such as a richly colored cut-velvet scarf so timeless that it might have been passed down to me by my own grandmother. And then there was a leather-bound, double-volume dictionary, complete with its own horn-handled magnifying glass. Using it always makes me feel like a total brainiac. And that's better than money in the bank.

More Than Just the Nanny

by Janet Carlson Freed

he day my daughter Erica called me "Ku-mommy," back when she was two years old, I took it as a signal that I had succeeded in forging a nearly perfect relationship with our nanny. Her name is Kumarie (Koo-MAR-ee), and she is from Trinidad. If Erica, who was an infant when she met Kumarie, could confuse us, then I could go to my office every day without quite so much working-parent guilt. It's possible my child didn't feel "left" with a sitter: instead she felt she had two mothers. Or, more precisely, her two caregivers were merged in her naive psyche as one complete mother figure, poetically named Ku-mommy.

Some mothers are jealous when their children call the babysitter Mommy or otherwise demonstrate filial attachment. I can understand that, but I myself didn't experience jealousy. For many of us, raising a child today requires dropping the barriers of the nuclear family. Our modern definition of the extended family may not include far-flung aunts and uncles, but it does embrace the nanny and the next-door neighbors.

I'll never forget the first morning I walked out the door and left my nine-month-old firstborn daughter, Alden, in the hands of a stranger, hoping for the best. Was I crazy? No crazier, I suppose, than the rest of this country full of dual-income families. For the most part, the caregiver arrangement works out fine, but there's no ignoring the fact that we're taking a gamble. I'm not alone in recalling with a shudder the 1990s trial of British nanny Louise Woodward whom the prosecutor portrayed as "frustrated, unhappy, resentful." Can any of us afford a baby-sitter who is those things? Who among us would not go to the farthest extreme, not just to hire the right person in the first place but then to do the far more difficult work of cultivating the best possible relationship with her? It's an unending project that calls on all the resources in our nature. Management skills are part of it, but just as important are the skills of humanity: empathy, generosity—all staples of good manners.

Thinking of the nanny, baby-sitter or au pair as family (since she shares in the responsibility for the welfare of the children) shows her the respect she deserves. She is, after all, different from any other "household employee" in that she's required to be your surrogate and look after what you prize most in the world. For her to do so necessitates that she bond with your children, that she indeed love them. That's asking a great deal of any employee. To me, the modern reality was that my husband and I had a partner in parenting—in our case, one who had raised three adorable daughters of her own. As a mother, Kumarie had ten years on me. That made her more of an expert than I. (Actually, I viewed us as just a couple of working girls.) I respected her work. No, that's too restrained: I worshiped the ground she walked on, because my girls were happy, and she made my life, such as I'd arranged it, possible.

> For many of us, raising a child today requires dropping the barriers of the nuclear family.

To say that things were downright collegial between Kumarie and me would be false and patronizing. I was the manager; she worked for me. But the delicate balance we sustained, between one good mother and another, was buoyed by a mutual respect for the gray areas of life and the calling of motherhood.

Although we had an excellent relationship overall, there were times when it was a bumpy ride. We struggled, for example, over grocery receipts. I'd give Kumarie a blank check and a list. I needed the receipt to mark the total in my checkbook and in case I had to return something. Often, there'd be no receipt on the table when I came home. It happened time and again. At first I was puzzled, then angry. Unable to sort it out, I did the shopping myself on Saturdays.

Then there was the daily diary our previous baby-sitters had been keeping since our daughters were born. Like any besotted mom, I loved reading it when I came home in the evening—what Alden had eaten, how many steps Erica had taken—and the sitters had all obliged. But I found I had to remind Kumarie constantly about jotting things down. I'd leave her those reminders every morning on yellow sticky notes atop the kitchen counter (our command central), to no avail.

Finally, one day my husband and I sat down to talk with Kumarie about why the tension in the house had grown so thick. Generally, in such instances, I think, people assume the baby-sitter is somehow at fault, that she's moody or has an attitude; we gave ours the benefit of the doubt. She'd come to us a shy, reserved woman, and we accepted that. Nevertheless, communication was needed here. Kumarie opened up at last and told me that she didn't like coming to work each morning to a barrage of yellow notes. Okay, she had a point there. I agreed to back off. But I stood firm on the grocery receipts. And we compromised on the daily diary by creating a weekly log sheet on the computer.

That was a turning point in our relationship. We became more tolerant of our differences. There is, after all, more than one way to load the dishwasher. And, I even came to see more than one way to raise my children. I learned to stick to these fundamentals:

- Don't sweat the small stuff. Tackle the major issues and let the rest slide, at least until the moment is right. Stand firm on things like safety, nutrition, and discipline, but give your nanny a break when she changes the settings on the car radio.
- Take time to listen (easier said than done) and empathize.
- Be generous with money (pay her more than the cleaning woman, for God's sake) and time (it's only polite to call if you're going to be late).
- Be flexible about vacation schedules (who can blame a woman whose relatives live abroad for wanting to take off two weeks in a row?).

Happily, there are times when things fall into place even without your most noble efforts. Such a time came for us one Halloween. I like to take that day off, because it's a major holiday in my family. It turned out to be beautifully convenient, in that October 31 was an important holy day for Kumarie's husband, a Hindu, and she had a big feast to prepare. So we gave her the day off.

Just a couple of working girls, dovetailing their schedules. I'm proud of the relationship we managed to craft over the years, and I expect Kumarie is proud, too. In her way, she would let me know. One morning, she told me, Erica looked around and asked, "Where's Mommy?" Kumarie replied, "Mommy's gone to work." And Erica said, "Oh, and you're here. I love you."

Tag, you're it.

The Forgotten Groom

· by Charles Dubow ·

There you are, standing at the altar with your best man beside you as quiet chatter mingles in the air with strains of Handel. Suddenly, the organist segues into the wedding march, and all eyes swing toward the back of the room. Necks crane eagerly as guests turn to see your wife-to-be—a vision in white lace and taffeta—begin her final walk as a single woman. She is a butterfly emerging from her chrysalis. Appreciative coos waft up from the pews. Handkerchiefs flutter expectantly from handbags and coat sleeves. In the excitement, you are forgotten; demoted to the role of supporting actor, you wait in the wings, Osric-like, while the star completes her grand entrance.

By now, the closing stage of your extended nuptial agenda, you've gotten used to being second banana. After all, you're only the groom. To some people you don't even exist—a nonperson.

After I was married, I went to pick up some of our wedding gifts. When I gave the salesperson my name, I received only a blank stare. "What is your wife's name, sir?" she asked, making me feel a tad oafish. Clearly, it was implied, I had no business being there in the first place. Wedding presents are a wife's domain, hers to choose and to collect. Men are allowed to come into contact with this newly acquired swag when they eat off it, carry it or break it.

If you want hard proof of the groom's lowly role, you need only consult the most venerable etiquette guides. Tucked in amid page after page of rules for being the perfect bride you'll find the occasional bone thrown to the groom. One book discusses him in the context of the "raucous" bachelor's dinner, leaving the sly suggestion that such a party boy couldn't be trusted with the niceties of conjugality. And the Emily Post tome devotes a whopping six pages not to the groom but to the guest!

Is it fair that a groom be accorded this inferior status? I mean, isn't he also getting married? Well, yes, but there are several important factors to take into account. One of the greatest differences between men and women is that men rarely dream about what kind of wedding they will have. Girls grow up fantasizing about how stunning they will look in their gowns and how dishy their future husbands will be. Boys are not programmed to think about such things. Instead, we dream of scoring the winning touchdown or owning a Ferrari. To be sure, we care about whom we marry, but, frankly, I've seen some fellows less enthused about the ceremony itself than they are about the prospect of scraping barnacles off their sailboats.

> One of the greatest differences between men and women is that men rarely dream about what kind of wedding they will have.

So it's not surprising that by the time you've been pronounced husband and wife, you, like most men, are not really sure how you got there (or, for that matter, why the bridesmaids are wearing such unflattering dresses). Of course, you remember proposing. That was several months ago. There was the ring and your new fiancée's tearful midnight telephone calls to her chums. There were the handshakes from your friends, family and in-laws-to-be, and a general feeling of goodwill in the air. But after all that, things get a little blurry: Once you pop the question, your role becomes largely cere-monial. The only thing required of you now is that you be on time (moderately sober) and have easy access to a wedding band, prefer-ably the one you bought for the occasion. Everything else, from the flowers on the tables to whether special chairs need to be flown in from Paris, is the responsibility of your fiancée, her family and, quite often, a professional wedding planner.

For more traditional weddings, it is expected that the groom willingly take a backseat in the preparation (an arrangement that, by and large, has elicited few protests among my male friends). This approach stems from a long-entrenched cultural chauvinism main-taining that weddings are women's work and that no self-respecting male would be caught dead helping his fiancée pick out china pat-terns. I know one fellow who literally bragged that the only things he knew about his wedding were the date and the ceremony time.

However, as society's strictures continue to ease up—leading to, among other things, a higher divorce rate among the parents of newlyweds—there have been corresponding changes in the groom's role. Rather than taking pride in their ignorance of the wedding plans, some men welcome the chance to do more than just "show up and shut up." So it seemed only fitting that I work more closely with my intended on our wedding. I participated in every aspect of the preparation, short of modeling wedding dresses for her. Much as I risk embarrassment by admitting it, I actually enjoyed the process. It brought my wife and me closer together, which in turn made the wedding itself more important to us both. A groom can go too far, though. I have a friend who, during the course of help-ing his fiancée plan their wedding, got so involved he tried to take over the whole thing. This irritated his betrothed so much that, justifiably, she threatened to cancel the works if he didn't knock it off.

For all the effort the bride and her team put into coordinating the affair, the groom still has certain formal, if relatively marginal, responsibilities. For example, he has to provide a guest list, a task that entails worrying about which relatives to invite and ringing up all his friends to find out what their middle initials stand for. Also, since weddings usually take place in the bride's hometown, the groom quite often must serve as an unofficial chaperon to his arriving family and friends. This may involve ferrying people to and from the airport, arranging for accommodations and gently explaining to Aunt Sophie why you can't have lunch with her the day before your wedding. Other duties include obtaining a marriage license, selecting a best man and redoing your will.

Still, no matter how much the groom does he is inevitably regarded as some good-time Charlie who's simply along for the ride. Maybe you've been up all night with your spouse-to-be devising the seating chart, but don't expect anyone to express concern about how tired *you* look. All sympathy is reserved for the bride; the best you can hope for is a hearty handshake and a "Good luck, son."

But since weddings are one of the last rituals that still bind us to our past as much as to each other, there is the urge to preserve what is most beautifully timeless about them: the white wedding gown, the cake, the bouquet toss, the toasts, the exchange of rings—all the grand panoply of the matrimonial celebration. If that means the groom becomes low man on the totem pole, so be it. As they say, it is her day . . . and good training for the rest of your life.

IX
WHAT GRACE DOES

*It lifts us beyond small-scale
possibility and shows us the range of good within.*

Something in the Way She Moves
· by Owen Edwards ·

here was a time when I fell in love with women for no other reason than how elegantly they moved. In the early sixties, as a young man recently arrived in mecca Manhattan from a small town, I was introduced by a friend to a secret source of free entertainment. In those days, the New York City Ballet, under the direction of George Balanchine, performed at the City Center theater on West Fifty-fifth Street, and the programs were usually made up of three or four short works interspersed with brief intermissions. During the breaks, members of the audience stood outside smoking and talking. My friend showed me how to mingle with them, go back inside when they did and slip into an empty seat in the theater's alpine reaches. (I won't defend this act of cultural larceny, except to say that I was only one member of a large group of stealth attendees tolerated by friendly ushers.)

What drew me back, night after night, was the sheer pleasure I took in the movements of the women onstage, from Maria Tallchief to Suzanne Farrell. Over the course of several ballet seasons (during which I sometimes even bought tickets), I must have had a dozen crushes on ballerinas. Yet I never hung around the stage door trying to meet any of them; I was afraid they would not be as they moved. I had no desire to have my elegant goddesses brought down to earth by the slightest awkward gesture or banal utterance.

Ever since those days, I've been fascinated by women who move elegantly. I'll admit that this might seem an exceedingly shallow basis for attraction, better suited to a time when a woman's value was measured partly by the way she enhanced a man's. But I've clung to my retro romantic fascination for a more substantial reason. Over the years, I've noticed that women who move elegantly usually do other things elegantly, whether speaking, entertaining or thinking. I have come to consider elegance a kind of intelligence: the outward sign of an inner equanimity applied to everything.

As is true of art, design and science, elegance is closely allied with simplicity and appropriateness. We are drawn to the elegant implements and furniture of the Shakers not only because they are so handsome but also because they are so restrained. A mathematician will praise an "elegant" solution, one that uses only the calculations required. When Balanchine's beauties moved across the stage, they captured the attention of the entire audience without obvious attempts to draw attention to themselves. So it is with an elegant woman: She enters a room and instantly becomes the center of interest without trying to alter the existing mood. She need not be beautiful to be powerfully attractive. She will inevitably do just the right thing without going half a step too far. Outgoing and friendly she may be. Pushy or patronizing? Never.

For all its appeal, elegance has no guarantee of safe passage through rowdy times. It's not like table manners. Elegance comes with no established rules, no blueprint for the exquisite gesture or gracious expression. Emulation, not regulation, is the wellspring of the fluidity one associates with elegant women. The stars of the dance world are known to a relatively limited audience, so today's

Elegance is closely allied with simplicity and appropriateness.

role models for elegance, as was true a generation or so ago, more commonly step out of Hollywood. That's a mixed blessing. Where are the Carole Lombards and Audrey Hepburns to set the standard? With a few exceptions, contemporary movie stars often appear to be clueless about how to get from point A to point B without a superfluous move.

In fairness, even the most rapt admirer of silver-screen goddesses understands that they are actresses playing the roles of elegant women. But it's important to recognize that many of these graceful stars comport themselves with equal elegance in their private lives and that we all can learn to enhance whatever natural elegance we have by playing elegant parts.

One reason for the popularity of films based on books by Jane Austen, Edith Wharton and Henry James, I suspect, is that audiences want to see young actresses in roles that call for a charm rarely in evidence during late-night talk-show interviews. Another reason, of course, is that we all seem to long for a time when clumsiness was still a social sin. In the world according to Jane Austen, the elegant gesture was all-important, and breaches of grace unforgivably bad form. (When Emma Woodhouse behaves shoddily by insulting a blameless acquaintance, the shock is seismic.) So perhaps the fault lies not in our stars, but in our times. Watching movies in which elegance is acted is one thing, of course; actually holding fast to elegance despite the demands of career, child-rearing and modern life in general is quite another. It takes determination—but, then, what of value doesn't?

There Is Nothing Like a Dane

by Jane Smiley

There were eleven questions on the dog intelligence test. By number ten ("When a desired object is placed underneath a low platform, how long does it take for the dog to begin reaching for it with her paws?"), our golden retriever Amber had already located herself in the 95th percentile. (It took her exactly three seconds to put her paw under the chair and push the ball out the other side, and another two seconds to whip around and pick it up.) So I opted out of question eleven, which required some elaborate construction of equipment.

I sent Amber over to my husband and called Hitchcock, our Great Dane. We went back to question number one. Hitchcock sat across from me, his ears forward, inquiring wrinkles deepening between his dark, kind eyes. I showed him a piece of meat. His tail thumped. I placed the meat on the floor between us and pointed at it with my finger. He saw it. I know he did. Then I showed him an empty can. He looked at it with interest. I pointed out the meat again. Desirable, fragrant meat. He whined one little polite note. I placed the can over the meat and began to time how long it would take him to knock over the can and take his reward (seven seconds for Amber—if the meat had been a ball, it would have taken her fewer than five).

Hitchcock looked at the can, then began gazing around the room. "No, Hitchie," I said, "look!" I showed him the meat again, then placed the can over it. He looked around the room once more. The seconds were mounting. "Out of sight, out of mind," I said. Hitchcock was looking at me now, mild and trustful, the meat as absent from his consciousness as if he had never seen it.

"He's just got manners, that's all," said my husband. "You put the can over the meat, it's your meat. He knows the rules!"

"He's forgotten about the meat," I said. "Look at his face!"

His face—square black muzzle silvered over; dark, silken ears; melancholy black eyes—turned to the Alpha Dog then back to me, full of questions, full of benignity.

Amber, sitting at the ready, knew exactly where the meat was. She couldn't take her eyes off the can.

"This isn't a fair test for him," I protested. "He's too good. He's not selfish enough!"

I picked up the can. Amazed, Hitchcock rediscovered the meat. But he didn't take it until I told him he could. Okay, so my husband and I were both right.

One of our dogs is a genius: Red-gold, beautiful and sleek, she can catch any ball in the air, solve any problem. She is attentive, affectionate, obedient and friendly. She is the perfect dog. But our other dog is a saint, an animal of such tact and noble demeanor that when we left him with a house sitter and he proceeded to have diarrhea all over the living room for thirty-six long hours, I kid you not, she loved him all the more. She knew he was distraught at violating his most deeply held taboo, and she felt the sort of respect for his feelings that people should always accord animals.

Dog adoration, I'm sure, is in the DNA, and I'm sure I was one of those babies for whom the very first sight of a dog was enthralling. I love their paws and velvety abdomens, their furry round chests and waving tails. Most of all, I love their faces, as different from ours as they are familiar: How strange dangling ears are, and furry foreheads and black noses; how odd it is that they have whiskers and arching, wolfish teeth, and yet how like our own faces they often seem—eager or dismayed, inquisitive or fearful. Knowledge, ours of them and theirs of us, flashes back and forth between our faces, as instantaneous as electricity.

Here are the names of all my life's dogs: Christie, Phoebe, Sam, Nutie, Daisy, Foggy, Hitchcock, Amber; cocker, poodle, vizsla, Great Dane (fawn), Great Dane (black), Shelty, Great Dane (fawn), golden retriever. Three at once is the optimum number. Even a small house and yard can take three (unless they are sighthounds and need to run), because three dogs constitute a dog society. A dog society spends a lot of time on domestic politics, and dog politics are as time-consuming as human politics. Three dogs working out who's up, who's down, who's friends with whom and who's temporarily on the outs not only gives them a more interesting life, it's also entertaining and enlightening for the humans. As Elizabeth Marshall Thomas pointed out in her book *The Secret Life of Dogs*, what canines want is not food, shelter or comfort; it's each other. It's only humane that they have what they want.

Dog adoration, I'm sure, is in the DNA, and I'm sure I was one of those babies for whom the very first sight of a dog was enthralling.

What I want, sometimes, is to lie on the floor next to Hitchcock, sniffing the top of his head. What Amber wants is to get in between us and push my hands away from him and onto herself.

I stroke and sniff and nestle against their furry warmth. The humans walk bipedally above us, impossibly tall, talking in distant, incomprehensible sentences. Pretty soon, we fall asleep. We are dogs.

My husband, always known in the family as Alpha Dog, long ago taught me the saying "Lie down with dogs, get up with fleas." He only wallows on the floor among the canines late at night, after everyone else has gone to bed. When we brought Hitchcock home from the breeder—a fully formed Great Dane in miniature—it was the Alpha Dog who won him over. The little guy grieved so for his littermates and his mother and grandmother that all he wanted to do was sit with his tiny head against the wall, looking at the floor. Wouldn't play, wouldn't eat, wouldn't drink.

Finally, the children and I went sadly to bed, regretful that we'd brought him his first experience of despair. The Alpha Dog sat up all night, feeding him bits of Puppy Chow soaked in milk, stroking that tiny head, tickling the bridge of his nose with one forefinger, whispering his name in the puppy's ears over and over. When the children and I got up for breakfast, Hitchie greeted us—bright-eyed, round and wriggling—and we were happy all day.

Under the best of circumstances, Great Danes don't last long. When he came to us, I thought eight or ten years would be a long time—long enough, maybe. But now I see his large absence looming closer. When I sit down, he puts his head on my shoulder, presses it against my ear and neck. I close my eyes and try to feel that weight so thoroughly that all it will take to feel it again in years to come is a wish.

When Daddy Was King

·• by Frank Langella •·—

I began the kind of bedtime story she loved most about the time she was four and her brother nearly six. He stopped asking for them at eight, but she insisted upon them nightly.

"How about two tonight?"

"No."

"Okay, three tomorrow."

"We'll see."

"Promise?"

Some nights there were four. Most there was only one. Sometimes none. I couldn't always dream them up. They were called "An Animal with a Problem" stories. An animal who lives in the jungle with all the other animals is born with a problem. A giraffe might have a short neck; a beaver no tail; a cat upside-down whiskers. When I began telling them to both children, my imagination ruled supreme, but as time went on, and her brother lost interest, I lost control to Sara. She named the animal, chose its sex and dreamed up the problem, sometimes sending the story in a direction all her own, and nothing would deter her from a happy ending. No matter how insurmountable the animal's problem, the story had to end happily. Snuffleupagus, who was born all white instead of pink and yellow, became, in old age, like all the other ones on "Sesame Street." The lion got back his roar, the knots came out of the tiger's tail, the blind monkey saw again, and a short moral ended the night.

Then there was the critique: "I didn't get that one." "That was too short." "That didn't make sense, Daddy." This said as she picked her pals from the platoon of stuffed animals on the three glass shelves behind her bed, lined them up against the bed's back rail, and interlocked their arms so that gazing over her as she slept could be a rabbit, next to a hippo, next to a puppy—a squad of fuzzy bodyguards. There would then be a Chosen One kissed, cuddled and wrapped in her arms for the night. But not before those arms reached up and curled around my neck so she could give me my kiss and hug, tight as could be.

There was no tight like my daughter's tight embrace. If I didn't gently try to break free she did not end the hug. She was there for life. Her abundant love overwhelmed me sometimes and evoked memories of when I had loved with that kind of power. When I had come at someone full out and leaped at their heart with all my heart. And sometimes during that embrace, my hand touched her little foot and the tiny three-inch scar left there by an operation to correct an imperfection at birth. A scar I loved as much as her whole being. And I knew our stories filled a need deep in her to be whole and normal the way every child imagines all the other animals to be. The stories grew fewer over time, then faded away as she entered the real jungle. But there are frozen images lined up in my mind—as permanent as my favorite photo of her, poised and ready in a white tutu and with me always.

She's plunking out her first piano lesson, her parakeet sitting on her shoulder. She's alone, sitting, having pulled her oversize T-shirt around her so that her arms are tucked inside and the body of the shirt fits taut over her legs, with only her head visible above a homemade little-girl tent. We're walking along the street. She holds my hand with both her hands, letting all her weight fully pull at my arm, sure that I will keep her from falling. Sometimes she's climbing on me, reaching up, as if my arms are branches, and saying "Shouldies, Daddy," as she sits on them and grabs my ears. When angry, she folds her arms in front, her lips pout and she literally harrumphs as her elbows hit her belly. If I wake her too early she irritably says, "I want Mommy." Or she courageously faces the first day at a new school, scared she won't fit in.

Safe at home again, she gets covered in wax making candles, becomes sick to her stomach eating messily made cookies, trashes the kitchen while making her mother breakfast in bed. Pillow fights, pajama parties, brother battles, wailing when the bird dies, lost teeth, first braids, racing through the house in a dress I'd bought her, looking back to see it flying behind and tumbling over the dog. Feeding the fire in the fireplace (saying, "It's going out") until it was an inferno. And each December 24, looking up at that empty fireplace for Santa as she left his milk and cookie: "Only one or he won't fit." And the turning-point Christmas when I asked if she'd heard him on the roof the night before and she said, "Oh, Daddy, that was you."

I remember saying, "Sara, you have a great brain." "Oh, yes, Daddy," she said, "I use both halves."

And when other realizations started coming to her: I remember saying, "Sara, you have a great brain." "Oh, yes, Daddy," she said, "I use both halves." Or, "Sara, all your life I'll always give you what I have." A beat passed and she said, "Can I have your watch?" And my favorite: When she was five, I took her on my lap and asked, "When you're all grown up and with children of your own, will you still come and sit on my lap?"

"Yes," she said, "and when you're dead, I'll sit on your grave."

While the grim reaper has not yet taken me from her, time and circumstance have forced a thousand little deaths. After leaving her waving from a window, I would sometimes find in my pocket at the airport a note: "I miss you so much. I love you so much." And when I came back, there was the leap into my arms; a laugh so unbridled it tore the heart; and the frantic search through my suitcase. She modeled the clothes, played with the toys, then disappeared to her room. Not, however, before insisting that in the morning I make her special breakfast: eggs with onions, bacon, cinnamon toast cut into triangles, and orange juice.

That breakfast has remained a constant in our lives, but little else has held as steady. Sara's mother and I parted. They moved far from where I live and her visits are too few. And now there is lipstick and eye shadow and secrets and long talks on the phone and a boy's picture in her wallet. And her impatient, "Oh Dad, please!" is no longer a question asking for a bedtime story. I'm the one at the door now as she leaves for the airport or packs for overnights with old friends—and when she goes there's nothing to find in my pockets. That hold-on-forever love in that hold-on-forever way has gone.

But the bittersweet freedom that comes with the empty pockets is more bearable with the knowledge that she seems happily joined with all the other animals in the jungle she now inhabits. And altogether sweet is the memory of that blink-of-an-eye time we shared, frozen, never to thaw and melt away, when Santa was a player and Daddy was a king.

Invisible Grace

by Owen Edwards

Ｎone of us can ever know enough about the intricate choreography in the dance of manners. There are always levels of the elegant game beyond those we've reached. People dedicated to honing their ability to improvise on the classic rules, adapting to changing situations and individual styles, always aspire to a master's level, a black belt in consideration. This is a genius for social equipoise so delicately intuitive that only those who've made the grade may be aware that it's at work. Often unnoticed, hence uncredited, such invisible grace is quintessential noblesse oblige. It offers its practitioners the deep, secret satisfaction of knowing things have gone well because of some perfectly timed action on their part.

The measure of all manners, of course, is how much they simplify and clarify life by eliminating confusion, indecision, distraction and awkwardness. Though no one can deny that manners spring from enlightened self-interest, they are expressed through generosity. At the master's level, invisible grace subtly enables others to be at their best, enhancing harmony by anticipating problems and eliminating them before they actually occur. Like a chess grand master capable of envisioning all the possibilities on the board many moves ahead, or a ballroom dancer (sometimes a man but usually a woman) with the capacity to make every partner feel infinitely smooth, the dispenser of invisible grace has an uncanny instinct for the rhythm of social encounters.

This anticipation is a gift, like perfect pitch. In a sense, it is a kind of perfect pitch. We all have inner tuning forks that vibrate to social signals, prompting us to make certain gestures before their absence would be noted. But for those who practice invisible grace, the tuning fork vibrates to signals at such a high frequency that few others can hear them. It sometimes seems they pick up signals before they're even sent. Urging the musical metaphor just a bit further, someone capable of invisible grace is like a great accompanist, happy to have hard-won skill presumed, about whom one can say, as did a *New York Times* review of a mezzo-soprano's recital, "Mr. [Warren] Jones played with his customary sensitivity."

> For those who practice invisible grace, the tuning fork vibrates to signals at such a high frequency that few others can hear them.

Acts of invisible grace are, by definition, almost never dramatic, since the whole point is to avoid drama. For example, some years ago, at a Municipal Art Society gala in New York, Brendan Gill, the late *New Yorker* writer, shared a temporary speakers' platform with several other luminaries. Beside him stood Jacqueline Kennedy Onassis, as dedicated to conserving the city's best architecture as Gill. The platform had no railing, and while the two listened to other speakers, Mrs. Onassis rested her hand lightly on Gill's shoulder. This might have seemed nothing more than a gesture of casual intimacy between friends. But Gill was by then beginning to show his age (while Jackie was at her ageless best); without drawing any attention to the act, the queen of Camelot was making sure that her friend stayed safely away from the platform's edge. The precaution was so impeccably camouflaged that Gill himself might have misinterpreted it.

To keep others comfortably within their own sphere of grace, no act of unseen consideration is too small. I remember lunching with a friend when I observed a couple at the next table whose interaction suggested they didn't know one another too well. Politely, the man asked his companion about herself, then listened with interest to her responses. While she talked, he ate, until he realized he was on a pace to finish his lunch while she was only halfway through hers. So he began to tell a story prompted by something she'd said, giving her a chance to catch up. As astronomers deduce the presence of certain celestial bodies only by their effect on others nearby, so keen observers will suspect invisible grace is at work without being able to offer proof.

This same kind of sub rosa concern to spare the feelings of others can be heard in the art of sotto voce correction. Let's say someone mispronounces a word in a group conversation—something like "nucular" for "nuclear." No master of manners would ever dream of correcting the speaker flat-out. Yet it would be equally unthinkable to let someone continue making that slight public gaffe and the tiny discordant note it causes. So a short time later (not too close to the mistake), someone—perhaps you—will use the same word correctly, with just a touch of emphasis, hoping that the only one who notices will be the person who needs to notice. "Isn't it sad, all these years after the Soviet Union came unglued, that the nuclear problem is still with us?" This act of shadow charity rendered, the secret sharer moves on, hoping for the best.

Those who act with invisible grace are like *The Scarlet Pimpernel*, hero of the romantic novel (later a movie), who, while maintaining his identity as a foppish English nobleman, makes daring forays across the Channel to save French aristocrats from the guillotine. Their disguises are so complete that one can only guess what they're up to.

Such stealthiness reminds me of an incident during a Christmas-shopping trip to New York. I was in line at a department-store counter just ahead of a harried-looking young mother with a toddler in tow. The child was fast approaching that witching hour when tantrums can hit like tornadoes. As his whining increased, so did the irritation of the others in line. Then something peculiar happened. A woman just behind me lost her grip on her shoulder bag, and everything in it cascaded onto the floor. The sight and sound were all the more spectacular for being unexpected. Attention that had been directed toward the toddler shifted to the woman and her accidental cornucopia. Another man and I, our slumbering sense of chivalry awakened, bent to help her. The child was mesmerized by the lipstick, compact, wallet, keys and assorted effluvia of the urban feminine life and the commotion of collecting it all. By the time the bag was back on its owner's shoulder, the relieved young mother was signing her credit-card receipt.

On the way back to my hotel, I wondered how a woman who didn't look as if she'd ever had a clumsy moment in her life could have upended her bag. Then I realized that something else had been going on. Risking her own dignity, she managed to avert a minor catastrophe that might have spoiled everyone's day. Cleverly, she'd saved the mother from the guillotine of silent censure while giving a couple of men a chance to feel better about themselves. What I'd witnessed was a splendid gambit of invisible grace.

Or . . . was it?